The Panfisherman's Bible

The Panfisherman's Bible

John Weiss

Drawings by
John F. Eggert

DOUBLEDAY
NEW YORK TORONTO LONDON SYDNEY AUCKLAND

PUBLISHED BY DOUBLEDAY
a division of Bantam Doubleday Dell Publishing Group, Inc.
666 Fifth Avenue, New York, New York 10103

DOUBLEDAY and the portrayal of an anchor with a dolphin
are registed trademarks of Doubleday, a division of Bantam
Doubleday Dell Publishing Group, Inc.

Library of Congress Cataloging-in-Publication Data

Weiss, John, 1944–
 The panfisherman's bible / John Weiss. —1st ed.
     p.   cm. — (Doubleday outdoor bibles)
 ISBN 0-385-42224-5
 1. Panfishing.   I. Title   II. Series.
SH691.P35W45   1993
799.1'758—dc20   92-29444
                                           CIP

Printed in the United States of America

March 1993

First Edition

Contents

Introduction

Here's a trivia question that is certain to open your eyes. What is the most popular type of fishing in North America?

Surely, it must be bass fishing. After all, there are entire magazines devoted to nothing but this particular species and every major body of water seems to host a bass tournament every weekend.

But if this is your answer, you're wrong.

Let's see, then. It must be trout fishing!

Wrong again.

According to an extensive angler survey conducted by the U.S. Fish and Wildlife Service, over 19 million Americans seriously pursue panfish, compared to 18 million bass anglers and 13 million trout enthusiasts.

But what, exactly, is a panfish? Well, first of all, the term "panfish" is a generic moniker that refers to a category of fishes which includes bluegills, sunfishes, crappies, yellow perch, rock bass, white bass, yellow bass, and white perch.

Moreover, there are several things all of these fishes have in common. Foremost, they all con-

veniently fit into a frying pan and they all afford table fare of the highest caliber.

Collectively, no other fishes are so widespread across the continent for they inhabit virtually every lake, reservoir, river, stream, and farm pond. Since every state in the union offers panfishing opportunities for at least several different species, no one ever has to travel far to wet his line, no matter where he lives. In fact, I'll bet that right now there is excellent panfishing of some sort within just one mile of your home, even if it's only a pond in a metropolitan park.

Since panfish are so prevalent, they are excellent prey for young anglers. If kids are successful on their first outings, as they usually are, they'll probably acquire a lifetime dedication to fishing in general.

This is certainly not meant to imply that adult anglers find panfish boring. When they are taken on appropriate tackle, so that they give a good account of themselves, feisty panfish keep anglers of all ages coming back for more.

Minnows are easily caught in a stream or lake by using a plastic minnow trap baited with crackers and submerged overnight on a rope tether.

1

Catching and Keeping Live Bait

There's no argument that when conditions are just right, a savvy angler can catch a heap of panfish on artificial lures.

Trouble is, nine times in ten, conditions are not just right. Maybe it's very early or late in the season and the cold water has made the fish lethargic. Or the water may be muddy from heavy rains, preventing the fish from being able to see their prey and making them rely upon other senses to feed, such as smell.

That's why, day in and day out, a great many panfish experts rely heavily upon live bait to add heft to their stringers.

There are many reasons why natural lures are so lethal, but heading the list is the fact that live prey is what most fish eat once they grow beyond the fry stage. Since panfish are used to seeing and capturing natural foods, what could be more logical than giving them exactly what they are accustomed to dining upon? Live bait also has the appearance, odor and innate action required to trigger strikes of its own accord, while an angler relying upon artificial lures must learn various presentation methods to impart the offering with lifelike qualities.

One disadvantage of live bait is that it can sometimes be expensive, or it may even be unavailable in certain areas or during certain times of year. Whenever this is the case, both situations are easily remedied by gathering your own bait and learning easy methods for storing it over prolonged periods of time.

CATCHING AND STORING MINNOWS

All species of panfish eat minnows at least upon occasion but they are eagerly devoured at every opportunity by crappies, white bass, yellow perch, and rock bass.

Actually, the word "minnow" is a generic term used to describe small fish such as shiners, chubs, dace, sculpins, silversides, killifishes, and darters, of which more than 200 subspecies have been identified in North America. A thriv-

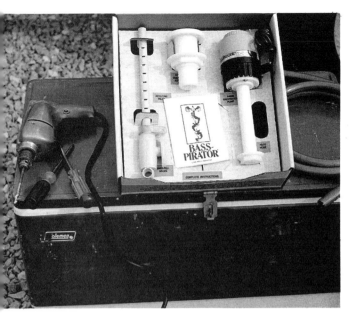

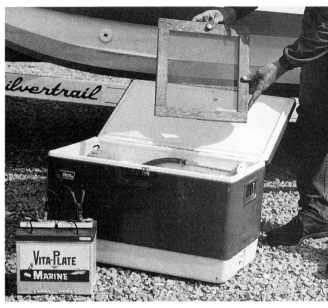

To store minnows at home for long periods, convert a camp cooler to a bait tank with an aerator.

A simple screened partition placed in a camp cooler allows you to store minnows of different sizes.

Aerator should be mounted inside the tank in this manner. Alligator clips attach to a 12-volt battery. If desired, an inexpensive timer can also be used.

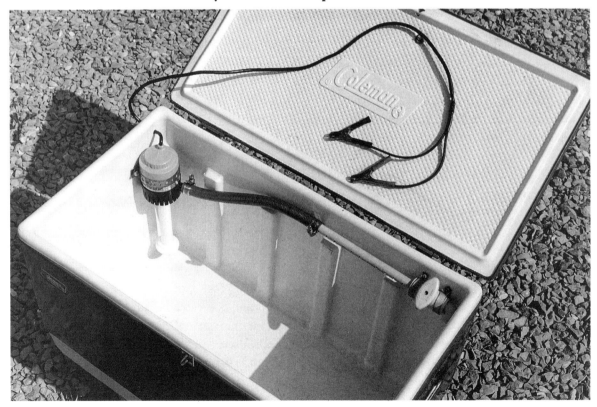

ing industry exists in which many different species are raised on enormous aquaculture farms where they are periodically seined by the millions from rearing ponds, loaded into tanker trucks and transported to tackle shops and bait stores around the country.

Despite the wide availability of commercially raised minnows, many anglers derive pleasure from trapping their own from streams, ponds, lakes and reservoirs. Just be sure to check your local regulations to determine if the practice is legal in your region.

The accepted method of catching the largest number of minnows is using a wire-mesh or clear-plastic minnow trap available at almost any tackle shop. Bait it with a slice of bread or several crackers, submerge it in shallow water on

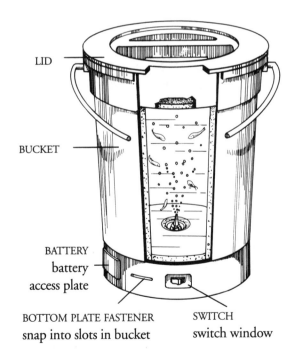

LID

BUCKET

BATTERY
battery access plate

BOTTOM PLATE FASTENER
snap into slots in bucket

SWITCH
switch window

For storing minnows in a boat, use a five-gallon aerated bait tank. This model runs twelve hours on a single D-cell battery.

a short rope tether, and the following day two dozen or more lively baitfish will be imprisoned in the trap.

Some of the most enthusiastic anglers who fish two or three times a week frequently trap hundreds of minnows and store them for up to six months in their garage; one year we calculated that we saved over $150 by trapping our own minnows.

The obvious question is how to store such a large quantity of minnows at home? We solved this by simply building our own bait tank. It consists of an old camping cooler outfitted with an inexpensive, 12-volt aerator of the type intended for anglers who wish to install such a device in a boat's livewell; a timer automatically turns the aerator on for five minutes every half hour. I even fabricated a screened partition to divide the interior of the bait tank. In this manner, I can simultaneously store two different size minnows, perhaps 1-inch crappie minnows in one side and 3-inch chubs for chain pickerel in the other.

Oxygen starvation, of course, is the number one cause of minnow loss, no matter what interim storage method is being used. Consequently, when minnows are transferred from a lake trap or bait tank to some other holding vessel in the boat, the bait must continue to have ample oxygen in the water.

One type of minnow bucket commonly found in tackle shops consists of a metal pail with a perforated metal insert that can be slipped over the side of the boat into the water and tied off with a length of cord; since the bucket floats at the surface, lake water continually circulates through the perforations to provide the minnows with all the oxygen they need.

However, I much prefer the extremely popular Aerobait pail. This brand of bait bucket is made of unbreakable plastic and comes in 7-quart and 5-gallon sizes, allowing either to conveniently sit right in your boat at all times so your bait always is handy. The Aerobait pail has

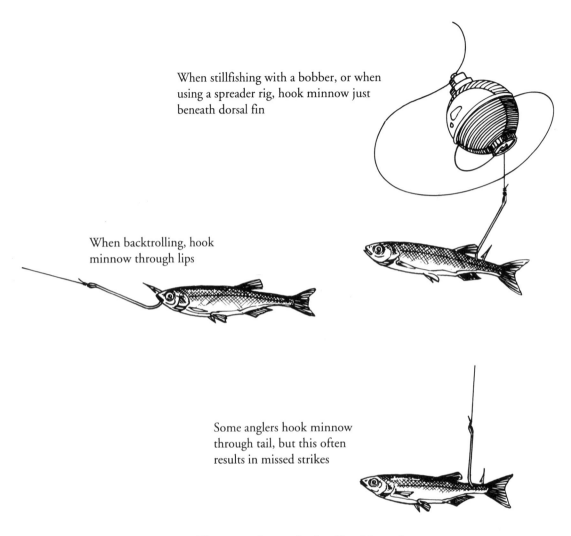

When stillfishing with a bobber, or when
using a spreader rig, hook minnow just
beneath dorsal fin

When backtrolling, hook
minnow through lips

Some anglers hook minnow
through tail, but this often
results in missed strikes

Three popular methods of hooking minnows.

a small, built-in aerator that runs all day on a single D-cell battery.

Fishing With Minnows

The manner in which a minnow should be impaled on a hook depends primarily upon the method of fishing to be undertaken.

First, always strive to inflict minimal damage upon the bait by using a thin-wire hook, as this will enable the minnow to remain frisky for a longer period of time. Similarly, since most panfish species have relatively small mouths, don't use a hook that is overly large or you may miss many strikes. Generally, hook sizes ranging from 4 to 8 will suffice for all of the panfish species described in this book—except bluegills and the sunfishes, in which case I recommend size 10 hooks.

For stillfishing—that is, hanging a minnow directly beneath some type of bobber—the best method of hooking the bait is just below the dorsal fin, but above the backbone; otherwise, if the hook is too far down into the body it will pierce the spine and kill the minnow. In vertically fishing without a bobber and using some type of weighted spreader rig as described in the chapters on crappies and yellow perch, it's best to hook the minnow gently through both lips as this allows it to swim freely in small circles and thus trigger more strikes. Hooking a minnow through both lips is also the recommended procedure when backtrolling a Lindy rig on the bottom, a lethal technique which also is discussed later.

Many anglers like to hook their minnows through the base of the tail, believing this is less injurious to the bait than any other method and therefore causes the minnow to exhibit a fluttering, distressed behavior that excites panfish and

elicits more active feeding on their part. This is true. However, since all predator fishes inhale minnows head-first, a tail-hooked minnow may result in a larger percentage of missed strikes than the other methods described above.

CATCHING AND STORING WORMS

I'd be willing to bet that almost anyone who looks back on his youth will agree that angleworms, red worms, and nightcrawlers were among the first live baits he ever fished. To this day, with graying hair, I still rely heavily upon worms, for the simple reason that they are highly effective in duping all species of panfish.

Additional benefits of worms are the relative ease with which they can be stored and transported, and that they are very inexpensive baits if you gather your own.

A little known fact about smaller earthworms, which also are known as angleworms, is that they are actually immature nightcrawlers. Otherwise, the different size creatures are both of the same species.

Although red worms are similar in size to angleworms, they are an entirely different species and favor a different type of environment, with a distinct preference for manure or decayed, rotting organic matter.

Generally, nightcrawlers are a bit too large for most panfishing endeavors, although they occasionally can be successfully used for larger panfish such as rock bass and yellow perch. As a result, angleworms and red worms are invariably far more effective, especially when bluegills and sunfish are being sought.

All three types of worms can be purchased at most bait shops, but it is not a difficult task to gather them yourself.

The most popular method of obtaining nightcrawlers is by picking them from neighborhood lawns after dark. The best time is after

Virtually every youngster begins his fishing career with worms, yet they are equally popular with adult anglers for all species of panfish.

Best way to keep worms at home is in styrofoam storage boxes placed in an old refrigerator in the garage or basement.

Don't use dirt in your worm boxes. Better is commercially made bedding mix which contains food to keep worms healthy and frisky.

a rainstorm has saturated the earth and driven the worms close to the surface. Keep in mind that nightcrawlers are very light-sensitive. Consequently, don't focus the main intensity of the flashlight beam directly on a crawler or it'll quickly withdraw into its hole in the sod. Instead, barely illuminate the worm with the dim, outer periphery of the beam or cover the lens with a piece of red cellophane held in place with a rubber band.

Nightcrawlers seldom entirely leave their holes and the single biggest mistake pickers make is grabbing a crawler and then pulling it from the ground too quickly. Often as not, this tears the crawler in two.

The trick is to press your thumb or finger gently against the crawler's body right where it enters it's hole in the ground. Don't press too hard! Then, with your other hand, grab the other end of the crawler. At first, it will squirm and resist, but in a few seconds it will relax and allow itself to be pulled from the ground easily without harm.

Immature nightcrawlers—angleworms—generally prefer looser, more disturbed soil. As a result, the best way to collect them is by using a spade to turn over shovelfuls of soil in a vegetable garden, flower bed, or mulch pile.

Red worms are best acquired by making contact with a farmer who has livestock and accumulates manure piles that once a year are spread over his meadows to add nitrogen to the soil. Meanwhile, such manure piles may contain thousands of red worms that you may be permitted to gather entirely free.

With regard to storing your accumulated bait, there are two things that will cause worms to wilt and die in short order: heat and excessive moisture. So it is imperative to make arrangements for keeping your worms in a cool, barely moist environment. Since the ideal temperature for worm storage is 45 to 50 degrees, it is almost imperative that one make use of some type of refrigerator. The best idea is to scrounge an old refrigerator from a used-appliance store (mine cost only $25) and put it in the garage or basement.

In making use of a small refrigerator, it is possible to store several thousand worms for a year or more. Although this seems like more worms than one could ever require, it isn't; serious bluegill and sunfish anglers, for example, commonly use six or seven dozen worms per daily outing and double that if a partner or some other family member tags along.

For storing worms in a refrigerator, I

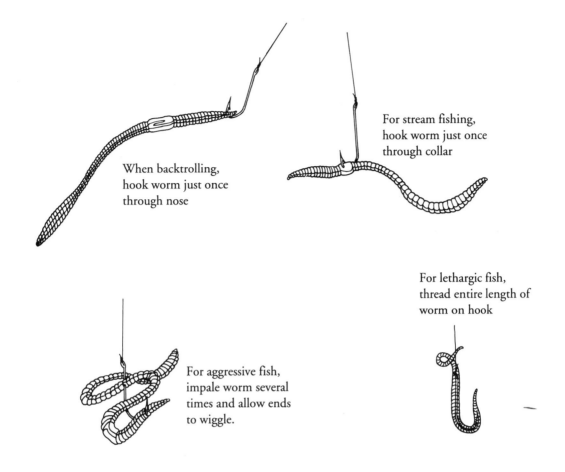

When backtrolling, hook worm just once through nose

For stream fishing, hook worm just once through collar

For lethargic fish, thread entire length of worm on hook

For aggressive fish, impale worm several times and allow ends to wiggle.

Four popular methods of hooking worms.

strongly suggest buying one or more large, commercially made worm boxes to house your entire colony and then a smaller box or two into which lesser quantities of worms can be transferred for each daily fishing outing.

These boxes generally are made of heavy-duty styrofoam, they have secure lids, and they measure approximately 18 inches wide, 24 inches long, and from 6 to 8 inches deep.

Although it might seem logical to fill a worm box with common dirt, this is not wise. Much better is purchasing a bag of commercially prepared worm bedding. The prime ingredient in most bedding mixes is either cellulose or sphagnum peat moss, but special nutrients also are added, so you don't have to bother feeding your worms. Follow the directions on the bedding package. They probably will emphasize that only just a tiny bit of water should be added, then the bedding wrung out to remove as much excess as possible.

In adding worms to your box, place them directly on top of the bedding. The reason for this is because there is a good chance a small percentage of your worms will have been injured when they were picked and are destined to die in short time. Consequently, the healthy worms will soon begin burrowing down into the bedding of their own accord; any injured worms will remain on top and a day or two later you can pick them off and discard them.

Your worms should now have ideal environ-

When fishing from small boats, or from the shore-line, a small worm box like this is ideal. A special flip-top lid ensures quick access to bait.

mental conditions to remain healthy and frisky for a long time. Eventually, the bedding will dry out. Never allow it to reach the crumbly state.

The proper way to moisten the bedding is to make a pad of several thicknesses of white paper toweling, soak it with water, wring it out, and place it on top of the bedding. The bedding will then very slowly wick the moisture away from the toweling.

Fishing With Worms

As mentioned earlier, in your refrigerator should be at least one much smaller worm box and it should contain bedding prepared in the same

RECOMMENDED HOOK PATTERNS

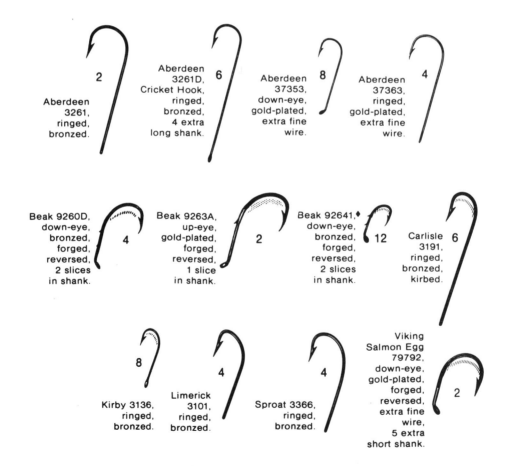

Various styles of hooks designed to be used with bait.

way as for the larger container. It's this smaller box that will accompany you in your boat during each day on the water.

When taking this smaller worm box fishing, keep in mind the air temperature will have a gradual warming effect upon the bedding mix. So always place the worm box in a shaded nook or cranny of your boat. Also, after an hour or two on the water, I like to take a handful of ice cubes from my onboard cooler, secure them in a plastic sandwich bag, tie the neck closed with a twist tie, and lay it on top of the bedding inside the worm box. The ice keeps the bedding mix cool, yet the slowly accumulating meltwater does not cause the bedding to become soggy.

As with minnows, a cardinal rule in fishing worms is to use the lightest, thin-wire hook to inflict minimal damage upon the bait and yet still be strong enough to hold the largest fish you expect to encounter. For panfish with small mouths, such as bluegills and sunfish, I generally rely upon a size 10 or 12 long-shanked Aberdeen; when a fish is caught, the long shank can be better grasped between thumb and forefinger for easier removal than a short-shank hook. For other panfish, a size 6 or 8 hook, in either a long-shank or short-shank design, usually suffices.

There are probably as many different methods of impaling a worm on a hook as there are anglers who use these lethal baits. Generally, I allow the feeding activity of the fish to determine the method used on a given day. If weather or water conditions are causing the fish to be rather lethargic, and they are barely pecking at my bait, I use the smallest worms I have on hand and try to thread them entirely on the hook, including the point, to ensure there are no exposed, wiggling pieces that can be nibbled off. But if the fish are aggressively inhaling the entire bait, I merely hook the worm once or twice, with the hook point again buried, and the head and tail allowed to wiggle free.

However, this applies only to stillfishing, in which a bobber of sorts is used, or a weighted spreader rig. When backtrolling with a Lindy rig, especially when fishing for species like yellow perch or white bass (discussed later), it is much better to hook the worm just once right through the nose so that the length of the worm trails behind with an attractive undulating motion. And when stream or river fishing for any panfish species, it's best to hook the worm just once, but this time directly under the collar so it appears entirely natural, as though it's being gently washed downstream in the current.

HOW TO CATCH, STORE, AND FISH LEECHES

Leeches are a favorite menu item of panfish, especially yellow perch, white perch, rock bass, white bass, and bluegills.

Although fifty different species of leeches are native to North America, it is the ribbon leech (*Nephelopsis obscura*) that is the most familiar to anglers, particularly throughout the northern border states and Canada. I suppose part of the reason ribbon leeches are so effective in catching the eye of panfish is because they continually squirm and gyrate in the water.

To collect your own leeches, you need only have access to a small lake or pond containing rather stagnant water. Fill a small burlap bag with meat scraps, entrails, or chicken parts. Put a rock in the bag for weight, then lower it into the water with a rope tied to a dock piling or tree branch. By the following morning the outside of the bag should have dozens of leeches clinging to it.

Since leeches are aquatic creatures, they must be stored in cool water. For long-term storage in my bait refrigerator, I use quart-size yogurt or cottage cheese containers filled two-thirds full of water. I put no more than 200 leeches in each and cover with the original snap-top lids. I change the water about once a week. For each

Leeches are very popular panfish baits. Hook a leech just once through the sucker on its head.

day's fishing, I then transfer one or two dozen leeches to smaller, half-pint plastic containers partially filled with water and store onboard in my iced-down camping cooler.

For those who decide not to gather their own leeches, they are commonly available at bait shops throughout the Midwest and northern border states. Those who live elsewhere should consult the classified ads in sportsmen's magazines as there are numerous bait dealers that ship bait nationwide by overnight-air express; upon delivery, simply store the bait in your refrigerator.

The two most popular ways to fish leeches are beneath conventional bobbers, with slip-bobbers, or by backtrolling Lindy rigs. In any of these cases, however, there is just one universal way of hooking the leech. Examine the leech carefully and you'll note that it has a harmless sucker attachment at its head, while the other end of the anatomy is a flat, pointed tail. Always hook the leech just once, right through the sucker, with a size 8 or 10 long-shanked hook.

The amazing thing I find about leeches—aside from their appeal to panfish—is their durability. I have frequently used the same leech to catch several dozen panfish over the course of almost a full-day's fishing before having to change to a new bait.

CRICKETS AND HOPPERS

Crickets and grasshoppers are premier panfish baits, especially for bluegills, sunfish, rock bass, and warmouth. It is surprising that throughout the southernmost states many generations of panfishermen have relied far more heavily upon crickets and hoppers than any other form of live bait, yet most northern anglers would admit they've never even tried them.

To catch grasshoppers, conduct your "hunts" during the early morning hours when cool air has made them lethargic and heavy dew has caused them to climb to the tops of weed stalks in open fields.

Crickets can be gathered under the same chilly, early morning conditions by lifting up boards or rocks on the ground around old or abandoned buildings. But a more efficient way to gather large numbers of crickets is to take an unsliced loaf of bread, hollow out a tunnel lengthwise through the middle, set it at the edge of a weed field, and the next morning it will contain dozens of crickets.

As each grasshopper or cricket is caught, transfer it to a half-gallon milk carton with a fold-over lid.

Throughout the south, crickets and hoppers also are widely stocked in bait shops, but else-

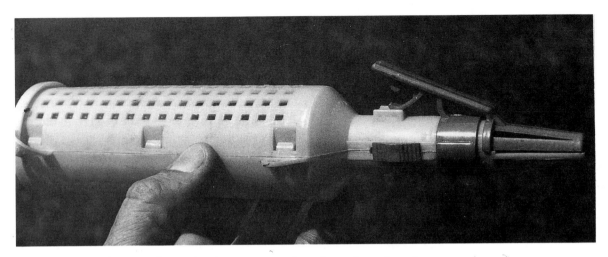

This popular cricket box prevents the critters from jumping out and escaping. One cricket at a time crawls through the narrow spout and is held for easy hooking. The lever is then depressed to release the bait.

where they are rare finds. So if you live in New Jersey, or Ohio, or Nebraska, for example, and don't care to gather your own bait, visit a pet shop; such stores commonly have crickets and hoppers because they are the live foods most often fed to pet snakes and lizards.

Home storage of crickets and grasshoppers is easy. All you need is a cardboard box or wooden crate with a screened lid. The bait will remain in good condition if the temperature range is 50 to 80 degrees, in which case the bait box can be stored in a corner of the garage. If the temperature is forecasted to dip below 50 degrees, move the bait box into your basement.

For prolonged storage of crickets and hoppers, they should have food and water. To supply their water needs, thoroughly saturate a wad of paper toweling and set it in a jar lid. For food, lay several lettuce leaves or a slice of potato in the bottom of the bait box.

In anticipation of a day's fishing, the bait will of course have to be transferred to a more portable container. I like to use one of the plastic, ventilated bait bottles especially designed to hold crickets and grasshoppers; they are available in tackle shops and through mail

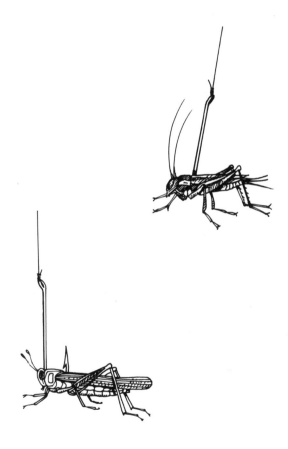

Hook grasshoppers and crickets just once through the tough shoulder collar.

order catalogs. The unique thing about these gizmos is that when the bait enters the narrow neck of the bottle it becomes trapped in a chute that gently holds it in position for ease of inserting your hook.

The universal method of fishing crickets and grasshoppers is beneath a conventional bobber or in conjunction with a slip-bobber. In either case, use a short-shanked size 8 or 10 hook and gently run it just beneath the shoulder collar with the hook point forward.

OTHER INSECTS

Other insects, in their larval forms, make splendid panfish baits, especially for those species whose daily menu is largely comprised of such foods. Examples are bluegills, sunfish, rock bass, and warmouth.

Many of these larval forms can be gathered on your own, while others are more conveniently purchased on a seasonal basis from local bait stores.

Maggots are the larvae of various species of flies. To acquire them, place meat scraps in a porous cloth bag and hang outside in a warm place. Flies will land on the bag, lay their eggs and within a few days the emerging larvae will crawl through the mesh openings to feed and grow by eating the meat. Simply turn the bag upside down into a cottage cheese container containing corn meal, secure with a snap-top lid, and store in a cool place. Fish the baits beneath bobbers by impaling two or three at a time on a size 10 or 12 hook.

Mealworms are nearly identical to maggots in size and shape, and are stored and fished the same way. The only difference is in the gathering. Mealworms are the larvae of grain beetles, which lay their eggs in grain. Thus, they can be gathered at grain elevators and feed stores wherever you find the remnants of old grain piles or spillage laying on the ground. Be sure to first ask permission to conduct your search.

Catalpa worms, which look like green caterpillars and are the larvae of various species of butterflies, are another superb panfish bait. Gather them in the spring when they build their gauze-like nests in the forks of tree trunks and branches. Place them in cottage cheese cartons containing sawdust and store in a cool location.

Catalpa worms are very delicate baits and so a unique method has evolved of hooking them that not only prolongs their usefulness but makes them "juicily" attractive to panfish. Take a long-shanked size-10 hook, insert the point lengthwise into the tail, then "unroll" the full body length of the larva onto the bend and shank of the hook, in effect turning the larva inside-out as in removing one of your socks.

I also urge the reader to take advantage of other larval forms that may be chanced upon in

When ice fishing, gather goldenrod stems from a nearby field. The bulbous gall contains larvae which are excellent panfish baits.

select regions from time to time. In many regions, waxworms and mousies, which look like oversize maggots, are raised commercially and made available in local bait shops.

June beetle grubs, which are fat and white and seldom exceed an inch in length, are commonly found when digging for earthworms.

In the dead of winter, ice fishermen often gather dead goldenrod stems from fields bordering the water's edge. Select only those stems revealing bulbous protrusions. Upon slicing open the knotlike bulb you'll find a wiggly gall worm, which is the larva of the wasp.

CRAYFISH AND HELLGRAMMITES

Generally, adult crayfish and hellgrammites are a bit too large for most panfish species to handle. But if they are captured early in the year when they are young and do not exceed two inches in length, they will eagerly be devoured by yellow perch, rock bass, white perch, yellow bass, and warmouth.

Crayfish and hellgrammites can quickly be gathered in a stream by holding a seine net stretched between two sticks. When a partner turns over rocks upstream, the critters are dislodged from their hiding places and swept downstream and into the waiting bulge in the net. Store them in a cool location in a small styrofoam cooler containing several inches of water and some rocks and moss. Then, for each day's fishing, transfer the bait to cottage cheese cartons containing water.

To fish these baits, use a long-shanked size 8 hook to impale either just beneath the shoulder collar; crayfish can also be hooked once through the meat of the tail.

PRESERVED BAITS

Finally, we should say a few words about the latest innovation in the panfisherman's world. This is the wide variety of preserved baits that have just begun coming onto the market.

While a fresh, wiggly live bait is the undisputed champ when it comes to inveigling large numbers of panfish, I nevertheless have had great success

Small crayfish and hellgrammites are easily caught with an outstretched seine net while a partner upstream turns over rocks.

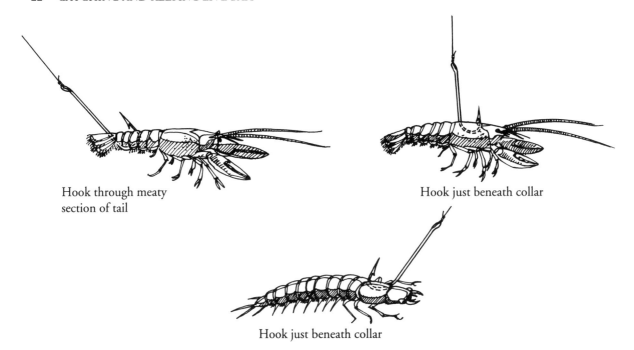

Hook through meaty
section of tail

Hook just beneath collar

Hook just beneath collar

Crayfish can be hooked through the shoulder collar or meaty portion of the tail. Hellgrammites should be hooked beneath the shoulder collar.

with these preserved lures. The Uncle Josh Bait Company, long known for its famous pork rind lures, has been the leader in this field.

Preserved baits are an excellent alternative when there's no bait shop in town. Or when you're traveling to an unfamiliar region and don't know what bait, if any, may be available locally.

Just a few of the preserved baits found on tackle shop shelves nowadays include minnows, shrimp, grasshoppers, locusts, grubs, leeches, crayfish, worms, crickets, hellgrammites, and caterpillars; these particular baits are generally put up in small, sealed plastic envelopes and are instantly ready for use. Others include maggots, mousies, waxworms, and mealworms. These are freeze-dried and put up in small tins. Just add a bit of water to reconstitute them to their original plump sizes.

Each of these preserved baits can be hooked and fished in exactly the same manner as their

A wide variety of preserved baits are now on the market. They are excellent alternatives when live bait is not locally available.

live counterparts. Try them all whenever you have the opportunity. I'm sure you'll be very pleasantly surprised.

2

Tackle and Lures

When it comes to selecting tackle for panfishing, anglers are extremely fortunate because the pursuit of their quarry seldom requires the same finesse and sophisticated equipment as might be warranted for trout, salmon, and other so-called glamour species. No better proof of this can be found than by visiting virtually any lake in the South and noting the preponderance of venerable cane poles still in use.

This is not meant to imply that shoddy equipment is perfectly acceptable for panfishing. The point is that panfishing should be fun fishing, with an emphasis upon getting the job done while simultaneously keeping everything as simple as possible. In that vein, forty years of panfishing have convinced me that all of the popular panfish species can be caught in large numbers with no need to overburden yourself with complicated technology or the most expensive equipment on the market.

However, there are some basic tackle considerations to keep in mind to derive the utmost enjoyment from your outings.

RODS, REELS, AND POLES

For the purposes of discussion, it's necessary to make a distinction between rods and poles. A rod is designed to cast a lure or bait and thus is always used in conjunction with some type of reel. A pole is not designed to cast offerings. It is made to dunk a lure or bait some distance from boat or bank. If a reel is mounted on a pole, its sole function is to store excess line.

Regardless of whether a given rod is of the spinning, spincasting, or baitcasting variety, the accent should always be on lightweight tackle and in many cases even ultralight tackle. Most panfish species are spirited fighters, yet since the majority of the fish an angler catches are likely to weigh less than a pound there is no logic in over-powering the feisty little scrappers with such heavy gear they are not able to give a good account of themselves. In keeping with this philosophy, the majority of panfishing rods best suited to a wide variety of tasks will range in length from 4 to 6 feet and will weigh from 2 to 5 ounces.

Fly rods, of course, will be somewhat longer, 6 to 8 feet, taking Nos. 4, 5, or 6 fly lines.

The next question pertaining to rod selection is whether it should be of fiberglass or graphite construction.

Graphite is a much stiffer material than fiberglass. Therefore, it gets the nod when the utmost in rod-tip sensitivity is required to detect very light bites and transmit those signals to the

The great thing about panfishing is that complicated, expensive tackle is not required to enjoy the sport and make excellent catches.

Best all-around fly rod for most panfish species is 6 to 8 feet in length, using a No. 4, 5, or 6 line.

hand holding the rod, as in retrieving small artificial lures such as spinners, backtrolling with live baits, working jigs on the bottom, or fly-casting subsurface insect imitations.

Conversely, less expensive fiberglass is adequate when you're using bobbers or floats with live baits, or casting surface-floating bugs and poppers. Then you can actually **see** your bites.

With regards to rod guides, I'll offer three important words of advice. For the best casting performance, a rod should sport one guide for each foot of length; therefore, a rod 6 feet long should have six guides.

In the case of rods used with open-face spinning reels, ensure that the first two guides closest to the reel (called "gathering guides") are quite large in diameter. Line comes off spinning reels in wide, spiraling loops and large gathering guides accommodate the coils of line with a minimum of friction, thus making for smooth casts and increased distance.

With all types of rods (except fly rods), I also strongly recommend selecting only those that have guides with ceramic inserts. Panfishing generally calls for very soft monofilament lines testing from 2 to 8 pounds. Such lines have

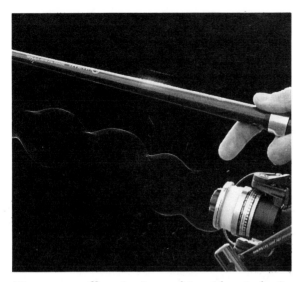

Line comes off a spinning reel in wide spirals. So be sure the rod you select has large gathering guides. For smooth casting, the rod should have one guide for each foot of the rod's length.

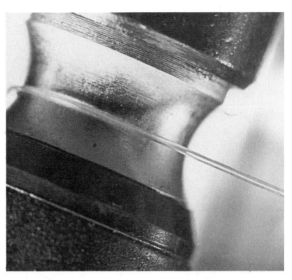

Frequently check to make sure the line roller on the bail of the spinning reel turns smoothly. If it stutters, it will cause line wear. A stuttering roller usually can be cured with a drop of oil.

minimal underwater visibility, do not overly impair the movement of a live bait or the action of a lure, and due to their limp nature do not stiffen up and snarl in cold weather. The disadvantage of such soft, thin diameter lines is that they are not very abrasion resistant and even the tiniest line grooves in cheap steel guides will quickly fray the line and cause it to part at an unexpected moment. Ceramic guides are very hard and smooth, thus prolonging the life of a line; nevertheless, still occasionally use a cotton swab to check every guide for signs of nicks or cracks that may cut your line.

But regardless of whether an angler's personal preference is for an open-face spinning reel, closed-face spincasting reel, or lightweight baitcasting reel, it must be matched to the chosen rod for optimum performance. These days, most manufacturers of rods and reels include cross-comparison charts with their gear. In this manner, an angler considering a particular reel can at a glance easily determine which of the manufacturer's rods are ideally suited to the use of that reel.

Occasionally check rod guides with a cotton swab to detect nicks which will cut your line.

FILLING A SPINNING REEL

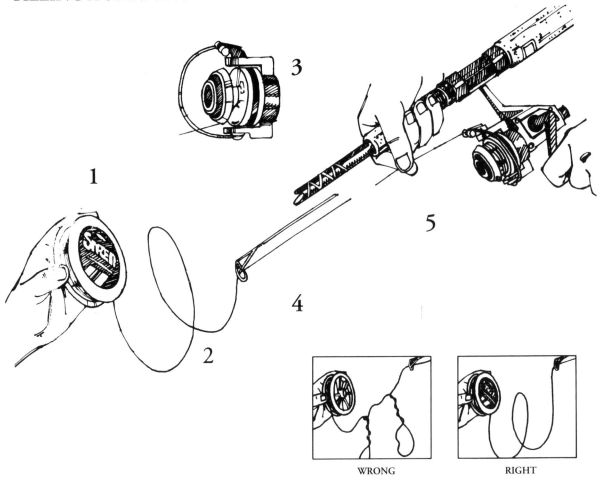

WRONG   RIGHT

When filling an open-face spinning reel, you must allow for the rotation
of the pickup bail which may cause the line to twist.

1. Have someone hold the supply spool or place it on the floor or ground.

2. Pull the line so that it spirals (balloons) off the end of the spool.

3. Thread the line through the rod guides and tie the line to the reel with the bail in the open position. Hold the rod tip three to four feet away from the supply spool. Make fifteen to twenty turns on the reel handle, then stop.

4. Check for line twist by moving the rod tip to about one foot from the supply spool. If the slack line twists, turn the supply spool completely around. This will eliminate most of the twist as you wind the rest of the line onto the reel.

5. Always keep a light tension on fishing line when spooling any reel. Do this by holding the line between the thumb and forefinger of your free hand.

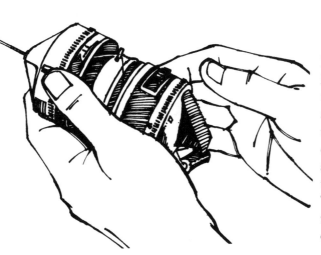

Filling a spincast reel: Follow the same procedure (steps 1 to 5) for filling a spinning reel. Remember to partially remove the reel cover so you will be able to see the spool and the rotation of the pickup pin. This is critical to insure that you do not underfill or overfill the spool.

Filling a revolving-spool reel: Insert a pencil into the supply spool to allow the fishing line to feed smoothly off the spool. Have someone hold each end of the pencil while you turn the reel handle. Keep proper tension on the line by having the person holding the pencil exert a slight inward pressure on the supply spool.

THE UNI-KNOT SYSTEM

Here is a system that uses one basic knot for a variety of applications. Developed by Vic Dunaway, author of numerous books on fishing and editor of *Florida Sportsman* magazine, the Uni-Knot can be varied to meet virtually every knot-tying need in either fresh or salt water.

Tying to Terminal Tackle

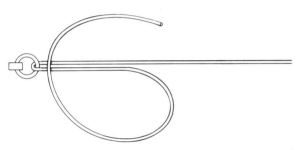

1. Run line through eye of hook, swivel, or lure at least six inches and fold to make two parallel lines. Bring end of line back in a circle toward hook or lure.

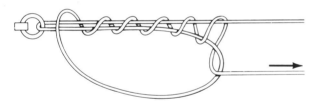

2. Make six turns with tag end around the double line and through the circle. Hold double line at point where it passes through eye and pull tag end to snug up turns.

3. Now pull standing line to slide knot up against eye.

4. Continue pulling until knot is tight. Trim tag end flush with closest coil of knot. Uni-knot will not slip.

Snelling a Hook

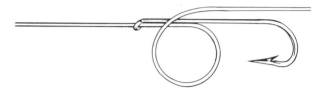

1. Thread line through hook eye about 6 inches. Hold line against hook shank and form Uni-Knot circle.

2. Make as many turns through loop and around line and shank as desired. Close knot by pulling on tag end of line.

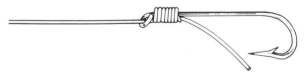

3. Tighten by pulling standing line in one direction and hook in the other.

Line to Reel Spool

1. Tie loop in end of line with Uni-Knot; only three turns needed. With bail of spinning reel open, slip loop over spool. (With revolving-spool reel, line must be passed around reel hub before tying the Uni-Knot.) 2. Pull on line to tighten loop.

Leader to Line

1. For tying on leader of no more than four times the pound/test of the line, double end of line and overlap with leader for about six inches. Make Uni circle with doubled line.

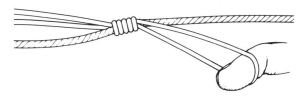

2. Tie basic Uni-Knot, making six turns around the two lines.

Loop Connection

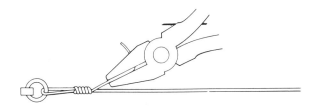

Tie same knot to point where turns are snugged up around standing line. Slide knot toward eye until loop size desired is reached. Pull tag end with pliers to maximum tightness. This gives lure or fly natural free movement in water. When fish is hooked, knot will slide tight against eye.

3. Now tie Uni-Knot with leader around double line. Again, use only three turns.

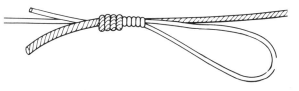

4. Use loose end of loop to tie another Uni-Knot and snug up.

KNOTS TO HOLD TERMINAL TACKLE

Improved Clinch Knot

This is a good knot for making terminal-tackle connections and is best used for lines up to 20-pound test. It is a preferred knot of professional fishermen and angling authorities.

1. Pass line through eye of hook, swivel, or lure. Double back and make five turns around the standing line. Hold coils in place; thread end of line around first loop above the eye, then through big loop as shown.

2. Hold tag end and standing line while coils are pulled up. Take care that coils are in spiral, not lapping over each other. Slide tight against eye.

Palomar Knot

This knot is equally as good as the Improved Clinch for terminal tackle connections and is easier to tie, except when using large plugs. It, too, is used by most of the pros.

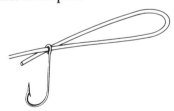

1. Double about 4 inches of line and pass loop through eye.

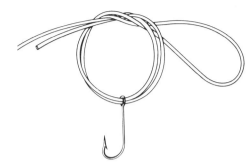

2. Let hook hang loose and tie overhand knot in doubled line. Avoid twisting the lines and don't tighten.

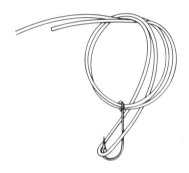

3. Pull loop of line far enough to pass it over hook, swivel, or lure. Make sure loop passes completely over this attachment.

4. Pull both tag end and standing line to tighten. Clip tag end.

In the United States, where most panfishing is done from some type of boat, panfish poles are usually 11 to 18 feet in length and are telescoped.

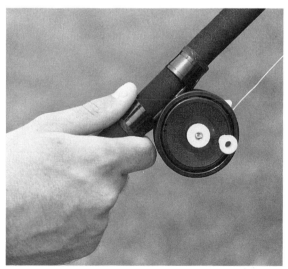

Throughout Europe, where most panfishing is done from the shore, poles up to 25 feet in length are very popular.

Most panfish poles are not used in conjunction with a reel because no actual casting is done. When a reel is occasionally mounted on a pole it invariably is an inexpensive model like this one, its only purpose being to store additional line.

On the subject of panfishing poles, it is intriguing that a European influence is spreading across North America. All of this can be credited to Mick Thill, of Great Britain, who has been teaching U.S. anglers many innovative ways to catch panfish.

Throughout Europe, tournament fishing has become an enormous spectator sport, primarily because there is little fishing from boats. Most fishing is done from shore, and an angler's versatility and catch ratio often is determined by the length of his pole. It is quite common, in fact, for poles to be 25 feet in length or more, thus allowing the fisherman to extend his reach far from the bank and gently place his baits with utmost precision in the tiniest openings in weeds or other cover.

On this side of the Atlantic, such lengthy poles have not become as popular for the simple reason that the bulk of our fishing is from various types of small boats, yet the principles underpinning their use have been widely accepted.

Most poles currently available in the U.S. are made of ultra-sensitive graphite, range in length from 10 to 15 feet, and may be of two-piece, three-piece, or telescoping design.

If a panfish pole under consideration is outfitted with guides, it is intended to be used with an inexpensive reel which serves the purpose of merely holding excess line. If no guides are present, a length of line equaling the length of the rod should be tied directly to the tip.

BOBBERS AND FLOATS

In fishing live baits for panfish, you can greatly increase your catch by selecting the proper method of suspending the bait at various depths. Many innovative designs in bobbers and floats are now on the market.

Consider the slip-bobber. This particular device allows you to fish a live bait at any depth (even 25 feet), which otherwise would not be

Bobber-stops, or slip-bobbers, are invaluable because they allow you to present a bait at any depth.

possible with a conventional bobber clamped onto the line. To rig a slip-bobber, first thread onto your line a tiny spring. Next, thread on a tiny bead with a hole through the center, and then the bobber itself, which is allowed to slide freely on the line. Finally, tie the end of the line to the hook.

Since the spring is adjustable, its placement determines the depth level at which you fish your bait. Moreover, the entire affair can be reeled in, with the bead and spring traveling right through the rod guides and onto the reel spool, and the bobber and baited hook traveling all the way to the rod tip. After the cast, the bait begins slowly sinking, with the bobber all the while sliding up the line until it is brought to a stop against the tiny bead, thus preventing the bait from sinking any deeper.

In choppy water, I suggest using a rig that incorporates a stand-up or pencil-type bobber, which is more visible from a distance, as opposed to a round bobber, which is better suited to calm surface conditions.

New balsa wood floats represent the greatest

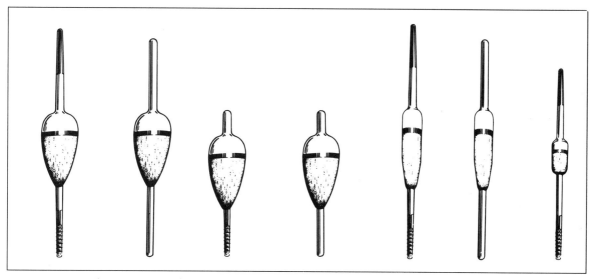

Floats come in a wide variety of designs that are perfect for panfishing.

refinement of the age-old cork bobber of years past and have dramatically improved catch ratios for legions of anglers. These floats are of the stand-up variety, with numerous designs for specific purposes. The rule of thumb in lake fishing is to select a float that has a low center of gravity, with the bulge below the surface and just the tip of the stem above the surface. Thus the float will not be affected by wind and the bait can be fished precisely where you want it. Conversely,

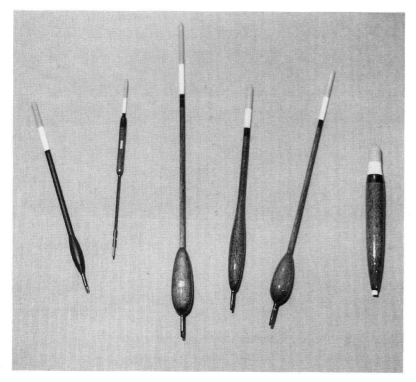

Experienced anglers rely on Thill floats for special situations like fishing in strong wind or fast river current.

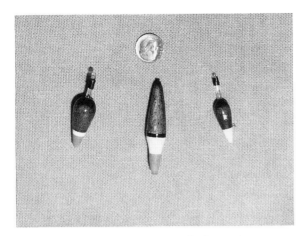

Tiny Thill stealth floats are ideal in calm water, clear water, or when fish are spooky.

for river fishing you would select a float with a high center of gravity, meaning the bulbous part

of the float would be near the surface, with the lengthy stem deep in the water to stabilize the float in the current.

FLIES, BUGS, POPPERS, AND JIGS

In most tackle shops and catalogs, you are likely to find an almost infinite variety of artificial lures designed for panfish.

Some of the most lethal are various types of wet flies, dry flies, and nymphs. And I'll confess that I always buy the cheapest patterns I can find at a discount house; my only requirement is that they be tied on size 10 and 12 hooks.

These lures are generally nondescript fly patterns put up by the dozen in blister packs by tackle companies you never heard of that im-

Most panfish species are heavy insect feeders and are not fussy when it comes to fly patterns. Inexpensive flies sold in bulk quantities are fine.

If it looks like a bug and moves like a bug, a panfish will grab it. Foam-bodied imitations with rubberband legs are excellent choices.

port them from Taiwan or some such place. But most panfish don't care. According to stomach analysis studies conducted by biologists, 85 percent of the diet of bluegills and sunfish, for example, is comprised of various insect forms, and on one study lake alone more than 260 different insects were identified. Thus, those particular panfish species that are predominantly insect feeders are invariably opportunists. If some small representative life form lands on the surface like an insect, looks like an insect, and moves like an insect, it's food!

However, if you are a discerning angler who is a little more selective, I recommend the Black Ant, Black Gnat, White Miller, Light Cahill, Zug Bug, Tellico Nymph, Wooly Worm, Adams, Quill Gordon, and McGinty Bee, to name a few. Streamer flies, such as the Grey Ghost, can also be used to take panfish that feed predominantly on minnows, such as white bass, yellow perch, and crappies.

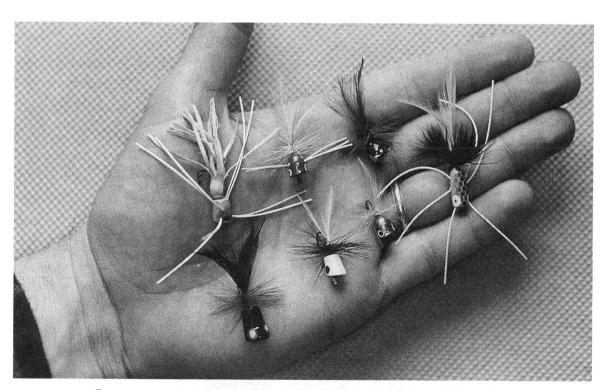

Poppers come in numerous designs. Small sizes are best for panfish. Different head designs should be considered for different water conditions.

When flyrodding from a boat, prevent your line from tangling on the electric motor's foot control pedal or other gear by draping a towel across the bow.

Jigs weighing ¹⁄₆₄ to ⅛ ounce are ideal for panfish. Buy a wide assortment of colors. Although a jig can be fished alone, dressing the hook with a live minnow will result in far more fish caught.

Plano's TackleRacker is perfect for panfishermen because of its removable, compartmented boxes, each of which can be used to store tackle for specific panfish species.

For fishing dry flies and wet flies on or just slightly beneath the surface, a level floating fly line is sufficient. Yet for fishing wet flies, streamer flies, or nymph patterns at deeper levels, a tapered fly line with a sinking tip section is far more desirable. In either case, resist the temptation to simply tie a 6-foot length of monofilament to the end of the fly line for leader material. A tapered leader with a 4X tippet is far better because the offering will land on the surface with minimum disturbance and thereby spook far fewer fish.

The term "bugs" is used to describe the numerous panfish lures designed to be used with fly tackle which represent crickets, small grasshoppers, and countless other terrestrials that may perchance fall into the water. For most panfish species, those tied on size 8 or 10 hooks are best.

I particularly like the many types of foam-bodied bugs with rubberband legs because they have a lifelike crawling appearance when slowly retrieved. Those in green, black, and white seem to produce best. These bugs are designed to be high floaters, but their sponge bodies will eventually soak up water and they'll begin slowly sinking. Simply squeeze the body and you're back in business. With such bugs, a slightly heavier leader is best; in most cases, a tapered leader with a 2X tippet.

Poppers are extremely exciting to fish because they also elicit explosive strikes on the surface. Generally, those weighing from $1/24$ to $1/32$ ounce tied on size 10 hooks are best. At a quick glance, they'll appear to have cork or balsa bodies about the size of a pencil eraser.

The shape of a popper's body influences its fish-taking ability. As a rule, use a popper with a concave, dished-out face for choppy surface conditions as this particular design produces a spluttering noise that attracts panfish. Yet in calm, flat-water conditions too much noise may alarm nearby fish, in which case a popper with a slanted or bullet-shaped head is far more productive.

Aside from this, poppers come in countless colors, some are dressed with feathers and yet others have rubber skirts. Keep a wide selection on hand and experiment to determine what the fish want on a given day.

Since poppers tend to be bulky and wind-resistant, I suggest using a stiff, level leader (a 6-foot length of standard 10-pound mono is fine). A stiff leader assures an extended shoot and curls outward like a ballerina's arm for a smooth lie-down, whereas a tapered leader used with such lures often collapses in flight and falls to the surface in a snarled mess.

Jigs likewise come in an infinite variety of designs. I suggest panfishermen stock a large number of plain, round-head jigs that can be dressed with plastic twister-tails or live baits such as minnows. Also in order are jigs with chenille bodies and marabou feathers. Generally, $\frac{1}{64}$ through $\frac{1}{8}$ ounce jigs will take every species of panfish described in this book. The most popular colors are white, black, yellow, chartreuse, and pink.

We'll have more to say about rods, reels, and lures in coming chapters as they apply to specific panfish species.

3

Weather and Panfishing

When anglers gather, regardless of the location or circumstances, you can be sure that heated debates on one subject or another are soon to follow. Probably the most common area of disagreement is how weather affects fish behavior.

For example, consider the way weather changes impact the underwater worlds in which fish live.

As the sky periodically clouds over, clears, then clouds over again, the amount of illumination in a fish's underwater world is altered from one extreme to another, thus determining not only its effectiveness as a predator but also its ability to hide from predators.

Likewise, heavy amounts of precipitation change the color of the water, either by roiling the bottom sediment in shallow areas, or by the sudden infusion of dirty run-off water through feeder tributaries into the lake, and this phenomenon can sharply reduce underwater visibility.

With changes in the seasons, and accompanying changes in the weather, water temperatures likewise fluctuate, and this governs the behavior of all fish by regulating their body metabolisms and consequently how often and how energetically they feed. On any given day, wind changes the surface layer of the water and this has a disorienting effect upon the movements of baitfish. Biologists believe that changing barometric pressure greatly influences fish behavior because it determines a fish's ability to adjust the volume of air within its swim bladder and thus maintain a neutral buoyancy with a minimal expenditure of effort.

COPING WITH WIND

There are a lot of cliches about wind, such as "when the wind is from the east the fish bite least," and "when the wind is from the west the fish bite best." But I suggest forgetting about wives' tales of this sort and concentrating instead upon the more realistic influences of wind and the practical aspects of making it work for you rather than hindering your efforts.

From my experience, the thing about wind that is important is not its direction but its velocity and therefore how it can hamper boat control and the presentation of lures or baits. As

When the wind kicks up, many anglers make the mistake of heading for quiet water in protected coves. But you'll catch far more fish in main-lake areas where lapping wave action buffets the banks.

for tackle, use gear that is slightly heavier than usual and lures that cast like bullets or are more streamlined and compact in form, rather than lightweight offerings or those which are full-bodied and fluffy. And rather than striving to execute long overhand casts, make short, accurate sidearm casts, keeping the lure as low as possible to the surface of the water as it sails through the air. Also, when retrieving the lure, don't hold the rod tip high. The wind will put a wide bow in the line and reduce your ability to detect strikes. Keep your rod low.

For casting live baits, use the slip-bobber rig described in Chapter 2 to make the terminal tackle more compact and wind resistant. I especially advise using one of the European floats described in Chapter 2; there are certain variations even called "wind cheaters" in which the body of the bobber rides *beneath* the surface, with only the upper stem visible above the water, which enables the bait to remain in its intended place rather than be pushed away by the wind.

Craft with high transoms and sidewalls and V-bottom hulls are the best for fishing windswept waters. This is one instance in which I leave my bassboat, johnboat, or canoe at home and fish out of a 14-foot aluminum deep-V. But whatever craft you elect to use, trying to position it with oars or a sculling paddle, in the face of stiff breezes, is the world's worst waste of time. You need an electric motor, and the higher the degree of thrust it is capable of mustering, the better.

If you're drift fishing, either with live baits beneath bobbers or randomly casting artificials to matted surface weeds, a neat trick is to set out a sea anchor. This consists of nothing more than a plastic bucket with a 30- to 40-foot length of rope tied to the handle. The bucket fills with water but maintains a semi-buoyancy and thereby acts as a brake to retard the speed at which you'll drift by potential fish-holding locations.

If forward trolling or backtrolling, execute your trolling pattern so that you're heading *into* the wind. This will allow you to control your trolling speed and turn on a dime, which simply isn't possible when the wind is prodding you from behind. When you're working a weedline, treeline, or other cover, it's better to move into the wind with an electric motor so that you aren't blown by likely looking spots before you've had a chance to fish them thoroughly.

Sometimes there is no alternative when fishing windy waters but to anchor. But be careful! Im-

In stiff breezes, avoid back-lashes and line tangles by making shorter casts, using heavier lures and baits, and casting in sidearm fashion with the rod held low and parallel to the water.

The Brush Anchor is ideal when fishing close to heavy cover protruding above the surface because the time-consuming process of lowering and raising an anchor is eliminated.

proper anchoring techniques, such as using an anchor line that is too short in rough water, can cause a craft to capsize or swamp. One method for failsafe anchoring is to tie your anchor line to your craft with a quick-release slip knot and tie an empty gallon plastic milk jug to the terminal end. Should the water suddenly become rough, just release the knot with a jerk and let go of the rope. The milk bottle will keep the anchor line afloat, marking the location of the anchor so that it can be retrieved at a later time.

Another technique is to use a device called a

Brush Anchor. This gizmo allows you, with a squeeze of the hand, to grab onto branches, limbs, roots or other cover above the surface of the water. The Brush Anchor was specifically designed for those panfishermen who like to maneuver close to standing trees, bushes, or other woody cover.

One other thing about fishing in wind. When stiff breezes kick up, many anglers immediately head for coves, canals, or shorelines on the protected lee side of the water where they can fish with minimum difficulty. Yet fish feeding activity is seldom of such intensity in these areas as it is on the windward side of the lake. That's because schools of minnows in such situations are unable to maintain their tight schooling dispositions when wind and waves buffet them one way and then the other. Panfish, especially the larger minnow-eating species, seem to realize this and move in to capitalize upon the forage's vulnerability. Even smaller panfish such as bluegills and sunfish will venture out from beneath the thickest weeds and brush cover, nose right up to the edges, face the open water, and wait in ambush for freshwater shrimp, scuds, insects, and other minuscule aquatic creatures to be blown their way.

THE COLD FRONT BLUES

While windy weather can be a panfisherman's bane or blessing, depending upon his knowledge of how wind affects fish behavior, the arrival of a cold front is virtually always to his disadvantage. To understand this phenomenon, I'll set the stage for the conditions under which fishing action for all species is by far the most favorable.

First, knowing that all panfish species are predators, and that predators prefer to lurk in shadows, I'd color the sky a solid gray to block sunlight penetration into the water. Perhaps I'd even hang an ominous looking thundercloud here or there, all of which would encourage fish to venture out and around the edges of cover in search of food rather than remain deeply buried far back underneath matted surface weeds or within the dark catacombs of jackstrawed logs or thick brush. There would be a gentle breeze blowing, but not enough to hamper precise boat control and the accurate presentation of lures or baits—just enough to put a light chop on the surface to increase the refraction of light rays. The day would be humid and hot. Let's say 85 degrees, with a relative humidity of over 60 percent. The water temperature would be at least 70 degrees, but no more than 80 degrees, because that is the range in which a majority of panfish species exhibit the most active body metabolisms, prompting them to go on the prowl for food. And the water color would be slightly milky, sandy, or cloudy rather than vodka clear. Further, all of these weather and water conditions would be stable—that is, they would have lasted for several days.

Under these ideal circumstances, even novice anglers enjoy good sport and catch an occasional fish. And veteran panfishermen do so well they are building upon memories to last a lifetime!

Now let's portray what I consider the worst possible fishing conditions. First, the sky would be pale blue in color, without a cloud in sight, allowing bright sunlight to penetrate deeply into the water. The air would be still and the surface of the water would look like a gigantic mirror. The water temperature would be less than 60 degrees and the air temperature would be noticeably cooler than just days before.

What we have described in this second example is a classic cold front, and under these conditions you can expect all fishing action to come to a near standstill.

According to meteorologists, a cold front is a line on a weather map in which the leading edge of a mass of cooler air is advancing into an area presently occupied by a mass of warmer air. Often, cold fronts are easy to identify because of the rapid drop in air temperature. But other times, cold fronts are almost indistinguishable because there is only a few degrees difference between the cold air meeting the warm air; nevertheless, the frontal condition will have the same adverse effect upon fishing.

However, it should be noted that the leading edge of a cold front can often offer fantastic fishing. An explanation for this is that advancing weather systems typically are associated with a prelude in the form of stormy conditions, such as the "excellent fishing weather" described earlier. But once this stormy weather has passed through, and usually for several days thereafter, you may have better luck getting your fish at the local grocery store.

Many anglers think the cold air itself has turned the fishing off, but that is not the case at all because it takes many days, sometimes even weeks, of consistently colder or warmer air temperatures to change the water temperature even a few degrees. Rather, here is how the behavior of fish is affected.

With the sky slightly overcast and scattered gray clouds beginning to appear on the western horizon, the fish begin moving slightly shallower or toward the outer perimeters of cover. The next day in all likelihood you'll see even more cloud cover and the sky will steadily become darker. Fishing action is beginning to intensify, especially during those intermittent periods when the surface is ruffled by erratic breezes. The following day the sky is saturated with dark thunderheads and wind velocity has increased somewhat. Now, fish seem to be everywhere and savvy anglers who know that this is a prime time to be on the water are loading their stringers.

Then the sky opens up, rain falls in torrents, gusting winds and whitecaps make it imprudent to be on the water and anglers bide their time engaged in other activities. Suddenly, a day or two later, dawn arrives clear and crisp. Nothing is stirring ... not even the mosquitos and gnats that were so bothersome just days earlier. You're thinking that this day it might even be a good idea to don a sweater.

Meanwhile, the fish, which had over a period of many days very gradually acclimated themselves to the steadily decreasing light levels, and moved shallower and shallower, are now suddenly and unexpectedly faced with dazzling brightness! They dive for the depths, swim far back underneath matted surface weeds, or find seclusion in the dark shade beneath logs on the bottom. And, curiously, less knowledgeable anglers who had previously stayed home, because the weather wasn't very pleasant, are now saying, "Hey, the weather is clearing, so let's go fishing!" And predictably, they catch nothing, except perhaps a few runts.

MAKING WEATHER WORK FOR YOU

By now, you may have deduced that there are several ways in which you can use weather to your fishing advantage.

First, make a point, every day, of listening to a weather report so that you can plan your fishing days in advance. As an illustration, let's say the forecast is for a mass of colder air to begin approaching the area in about five days. The best strategy in this case would be to wait three days before taking time off to go fishing. Then you'll be on the water for two cloudy days just prior to the arrival of the frontal system.

As another example, for those who are free only on weekends, let's say it's Friday night and you plan to go fishing all day Saturday. You want to try a particular lake that is about fifty miles from your home and to the west. That evening you tune in the weather forecast and learn that a cold front is rapidly descending upon the region and will probably arrive sometime during the night or perhaps the following morning.

In this situation it would be a big mistake to follow through with your previous plans because upon arriving at the lake to the west of your home you'd be greeted with cold front conditions. It would be much wiser to select an alternate fishing site located to the east of your home.

Many dedicated anglers who are knowledgeable about weather often climb out of the sack at 3 a.m. and drive eastward as much as 100 miles or more, with some particular lake in mind, in order to get ahead of the leading edge of a frontal system, rather than fish closer to home under post-frontal conditions.

Sometime this year, however, you'll have little choice but to fish during cold-front conditions. Maybe you'll be on vacation, at some fishing camp, and since you've traveled far and invested

Cold-front conditions turn fish off. Now is the time to fish right on the bottom wherever there are deep rocks, logs, stumps, or weeds.

a lot of money it would be a losing proposition to pack up and head for home. What you need in such cases is a special bag of tricks.

First, keep in mind that most panfish species will no longer be lurking near the outer edges and perimeters of cover. They will be buried in the cover, far back underneath a canopy of dense vegetation, within the crowns of trees lying on the bottom, in the shade of underwater ledge outcroppings, beneath jumbled log formations on the bottom, or wherever else they can find seclusion. Undoubtedly, the fish will also be somewhat deeper than in previous days. And they will be feeding lethargicly.

There is a three-pronged method to combat the negative influence of weather systems that have turned fish off. Fish dark water, fish on or near the bottom, and fish with live baits.

The best way to do this is with a long telescoping panfish pole with which you can reach out and enticingly dabble worms, crickets, minnows, and similar baits in the tiniest pothole openings in the thickest cover you can find. No matter what the water depth happens to be, adjust your bobber, or use a slip-bobber, so the offering is presented near the bottom. And be ever vigilant in watching your bobber because any bites you receive will be barely perceptible pecks. Give the fish plenty of time to mouth the offering; he may briefly inhale it, quickly eject it, then moments later gingerly take it still again, so don't be too eager to set the hook until you're confident he has committed himself to entirely taking the bait.

Don't expect to catch a lot of fish in this manner and under these conditions. At best, you'll get one here, another somewhere else, but it sure beats scrapping the outing and going home.

MORE WEATHER TIPS

Although the arrival of a cold front can abruptly shut down fishing in a matter of just a few hours, it should be noted that weather patterns often stall in a region for days or even weeks at a time. This phenomenon can give birth to the type of fast action anglers' dreams are made of, despite the fact that the weather and water conditions may superficially appear to resemble nothing more than a prolonged cold front.

This brings us back to what we said at the beginning of this chapter about the condition most conducive to fish activity: *stability.* Don't make the mistake of thinking stability necessarily means calm, settled weather. In the context in which it is used here, stability refers to *consistency* over a period of at least three days.

Therefore, a three-day stable weather pattern could mean three days of clear skies and gusting winds, three days of overcast skies and drizzling rainfall, three days of muggy weather under a scorching hot sun, or even three days of bone-chilling cold weather. What is important is not the specific character of the weather but the fact that it occurs without interruption for at least three consecutive days.

This three-day period gives panfish time to acclimate themselves to the changes in their environments that ushered in the period and to begin a slow and steady recovery to their former levels of activity. Hence, beginning with the *fourth* day after a significant change in the weather, fishing should be terrific. And it should stay that way, at least until such time as the weather once again changes abruptly.

Another tip to keep in mind when faced with a cold front or unstable weather is to fish a large river instead of a lake. The primary thing that distinguishes a river from a lake (or reservoir or pond) is the presence of current. This means the water almost always has a noticeable degree of color to it and its creatures are thereby less sensitive to abruptly changing weather conditions. A river's current also is continually homogenizing the water in terms of its temperature, dissolved oxygen content, pH and other components, which affords still another level of stability for the fish.

When weather conditions bring a halt to feeding behavior of panfish living in lakes, switch to rivers or streams where ever-present current negates the effect of weather.

Many times, I've found myself fishing a favorite lake with good success and upon the arrival of a frontal system immediately switched to a river and continued to make excellent catches while my pals, doggedly determined to stay at the lake, saw their catches rapidly diminish.

Finally, yet another trick in the panfisherman's arsenal is recognizing the fact that some fish species are more temperamental than others when it comes to changes in their environ-ments. So if your particular locale does not offer the opportunity during unstable weather conditions to fish a river instead of a lake, seriously consider targeting a different species.

Crappies, white bass, bluegills, and especially yellow perch seem to be the first to exhibit reduced activity levels at even a hint of major changes in the offing. If you've been after one of these particular species, and find it necessary to fish under cold front conditions, consider switching to rock bass, sunfish, or chain pickerel.

4

Meet the Bluegill

The bluegill is unquestionably America's most popular panfish, and with good reason. Its widespread distribution makes it easily accessible to anglers in every state. Moreover, within each state it does not occupy a restricted habitat niche like many other species but can be found in virtually every warmwater stream, river, pond, lake, and reservoir. In fact, in most bodies of water bluegills are so prolific that biologists say it's in the best interests of the species for fishermen to keep all they can make good use of, which means anglers commonly make very large catches without worrying about harming the resource.

However, none of this is meant to imply that bluegills are pushovers. Those anglers who are the most successful in consistently catching large numbers of these tasty panfish have learned as much as possible about the habits of the species.

Bluegills are members of the large family known as sunfishes. Biologists refer to the species as *Lepomis macrochirus* but throughout the South it's common to hear them called *bream* (or *brim*) which is entirely incorrect for the true bream is found only in Europe.

Originally native to the Mississippi, Great Lakes, and Eastern Seaboard drainage basin, the bluegill's range has been so enlarged in the past century that the species now inhabits every state and portions of Canada and Mexico. The only places where bluegills are conspicuously absent are at high altitudes in the Rocky Mountain states

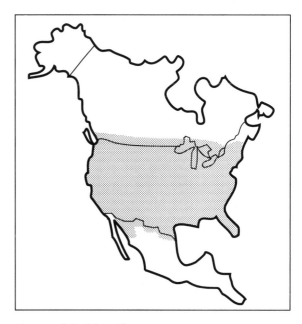

Range of the bluegill.

In many bodies of water, true-strain bluegills can be difficult to identify because they commonly hybridize with other members of the sunfish family.

where the year-round water temperature is too cool to support anything but trout, char, and whitefish.

In some bodies of water, bluegills can be difficult to identify, the reason being that they commonly mate (hybridize) with other sunfishes to which they are closely related and this results in body features and markings of both parents.

Nevertheless, in waters where pure-strain bluegills are prevalent, certain distinguishing features readily tell the angler exactly what he has caught. As their description suggests, bluegills have a light-blue gill cover. The round ear flap is nearly always solid black and the head is short, with a pugged mouth. The dorsal region is dark olive and the sides shade to a lighter, silvery-olive or pale green accentuated by numerous, dark-brown vertical diamond shapes. In many regions of the country the species also has five or six dark vertical bands along its sides. During the spawning season, males have a vivid blue head and throat and a bright coppery-orange breast, while females have yellow breasts.

Despite this wide range of color variations and design markings, there are two features which clearly distinguish bluegills from other sunfishes: a three-spined anal fin and a black blotch at the rearmost part of the dorsal fin.

The average adult bluegill an angler is likely to catch will be approximately 8 inches in length and weigh ½ pound, with the most sought after prizes being so-called "pounders" that average 11 inches.

Interestingly, as bluegills grow still larger, they do not extend their body growth very much in length but rather in height and body thickness (particularly breadth across the shoulders). As evidence of this, the world-record 4-pound, 12-ounce bluegill caught in Alabama in 1950 measured only 14 inches long.

It's this unique anatomy that makes adult bluegills such spirited fighters. Once they take a lure or bait, they turn sideways at a right angle to the direction of pull to allow water resistance against their broad, flat sides to work to their advantage. Indeed, many anglers have speculated that if bluegills ever grew to 10 pounds fishermen would require saltwater tackle to land them.

In the bodies of water they inhabit, bluegills are residents of the shallows throughout most of the year. Furthermore, they prefer little or no current, which means that in streams and rivers they'll be found almost exclusively in quiet, sluggish sections or wherever dense cover, such as a fallen tree along the bank, greatly retards the flow of water.

Otherwise, in lakes, reservoirs, and large ponds, the fish are found in greatest numbers in creek arms, large protected embayments and sheltered coves, sloughs, marshes, and inundated swamps. At certain times of year, as will be discussed later, they can also be found in main-lake areas but usually only in conjunction with heavily matted weed growth, thick brush cover, flooded forests, or certain types of bottom configurations such as rock-strewn bars.

FEEDING HABITS OF BLUEGILLS

All of the sunfishes, including bluegills, fall midway in the trophic food chain, meaning that they prey upon a wide variety of food items while simultaneously themselves serving as forage for still larger fish species.

As noted in Chapter 2, 85 percent of the bluegill's diet consists of insect life. Just a few of its favorites: all life stages (larva, juveniles, and

Bluegills inhabit shallow water much of the year, where they feed primarily upon insects. They'll hit artificials greedily and put up a good fight.

Bluegills like to ease up to an insect and watch it for a moment before striking, so don't retrieve a lure too fast.

adults) of dragonflies, damselflies, caddisflies, aquatic beetles, midges, crickets, grasshoppers, mosquitos, and water spiders.

An additional 10 percent of the bluegill's diet includes grubs, freshwater shrimp, tiny crayfish, snails, and earthworms that wash into the water during rainstorms. Only 5 percent of its food consists of other fish. Because of its small mouth, these are invariably pin minnows and the newly hatched fry of other species which have not yet exceeded an inch or so in length.

Given this, it stands to reason the accomplished bluegill angler will undoubtedly be one who has mastered the use of fly tackle and a wide variety of surface and subsurface insect im-

itations, or light spinning tackle with assorted live baits such as crickets, mealworms, wax worms, earthworms and the like.

Another vitally important thing to keep in mind is that bluegills rarely engage in chase-and-catch feeding behavior. They do like their intended prey to exhibit some semblance of life but if it is moving along quickly through the water, chances are it will be ignored. More often, a bluegill will spot a potential food item, rush in close, come to an abrupt halt mere inches away, and then suspiciously observe the prey for long moments. Only when the bluegill is convinced the food is genuine will it dart those last few inches to inhale the subsurface offering,

or casually rise and slurp it off the surface, and then quickly turn and swim away.

Yet if a bluegill discovers he has been duped with a counterfeit, he'll eject it in an instant. Therefore, no matter what type of tackle you may be using, always keep the slack out of your line and be ready to set the hook quickly.

FINDING THE SPRING SPAWNERS

There's little question the largest numbers of fish that bluegill anglers are likely to catch, and the largest individual specimens, will be taken during the spring spawning period when the fish congregate in certain areas to engage in nest building and the rearing of the current year's young.

In the case of some other fish species, such as largemouth bass for example, fishing spawning beds is often looked upon with disfavor because it can seriously deplete the resource. But bluegills (and most other sunfish species) tend to reproduce themselves in such staggering numbers that it is imperative they be regularly thinned out. If not, the fish will quickly outrun their available food supply, resulting in future generations which are stunted. Moreover, a body of water overpopulated with stunted panfish can decimate other fish species such as bass by devouring their eggs and newly hatched fry.

Bluegill spawning behavior is regulated by water temperature. Generally, the fish remain in their deep-water winter patterns until the shallows consistently remain at 65 degrees. Then they climb from their nearby creek channel holding locations, or rise from the edges of steep drop-offs, and venture toward nesting

In the spring, look for spawning bluegills in the shallowest regions of a lake, especially where brush cover is present.

grounds to repeat a mating performance that is as old as time.

The first places bluegills make their appearances are the backends of shallow embayments, creek arms, and canals. But if a lake or pond in question possesses numerous such locations, here is a short-cut worth noting in finding spawning beds. Investigate those particular spots known to have a soft muddy or marshy bottom. Compared to hard-bottoms, mucky bottoms absorb rather than reflect radiating sunlight and are thus much warmer and the first places where spawning activity occurs. If there is evidence of light brush cover on the bottom, or the exposed root masses of nearby standing trees, all the better.

I like to look for shoreline willows, pines, and other trees with branches overhanging the water because these species hint at the likely bottom composition. Willows, for example, grow primarily in soft soil while conifers dote upon sand and gravel. Bluegills do not nest far back underneath outstretched branches in deep shade — they prefer at least some sunlight—yet they seem to know that sparse overhanging branches will provide them with a cornucopia of free eats as the wind periodically rustles the limbs and dislodges insect life.

It should also be noted that throughout the deep South, where bodies of water do not freeze over and where water temperatures may remain relatively warm even during the dead of winter, it has been learned that various percentages of the inhabiting bluegill population may engage in spawning behavior throughout the entire course of the year.

Even north of the Mason-Dixon line, adult bluegills may spawn once in May, a second time in July, and in rare instances still a third time in September, especially if a given year's weather is unusually warm. I mention this because no matter where an angler lives, he should keep tabs on the very shallowest areas of his favorite body of water in hopes of being the beneficiary of a resurgence of spawning activity long after the initial spring mating period is over.

It's also worth mentioning that bluegills, like all sunfishes, have a strong homing instinct. Therefore, since ideal bedding locations in any body of water are usually at a premium, they can be expected to see use year after year. So remember where you find spawning beds this year and revisit those same places next year.

The spawning beds themselves are relatively easy to recognize, especially if the water is not overly murky. They appear as light-colored, saucer-shaped depressions averaging from 6 to

15 inches in diameter in water typically less than 3 feet deep. Moreover, bluegills are known as "colonial" spawners, which means they habitually gather in large numbers in very specific areas. The bottoms of these places often take on a massive honeycombed appearance. Consequently, while you'll always want to cast your offering toward the incidental clusters of two or three spawning beds you may find here and there, try to locate large colonies of nesting sites where there may be several dozen beds.

Like most panfish species, it is the male bluegill which is charged with the responsibility of housekeeping during the spawning period. He is the one that first ventures into the shallows to sweep away a nesting site. The female then briefly visits the bed and deposits her eggs while the male simultaneously fertilizes them. The female then retreats into slightly deeper water while the male stands guard, alternately fanning the water to keep sediment in suspension (which otherwise would settle and suffocate the eggs) and chasing away interlopers hoping for an easy meal.

CATCHING SPAWNING BLUEGILLS

If you fish a spawning bed, you're likely to catch both males and females. Sometimes you'll catch only males. At any rate, both males and females are extremely aggressive when on or near their nests and this means you need not be overly selective in your choice of baits or lures.

In fact, catching spawning bluegills is typically so fast and action-packed that most anglers don't even bother with the time-consuming chore of hooking live bait. But for those who prefer bait-fishing, there are two techniques that are most effective.

The first is using a 12- to 14-foot panfish pole, with or without an inexpensive reel taped to the handle. Some of the most experienced bluegill anglers even opt in favor of a telescoping or take-apart European-style panfish pole up to 18 feet in length, as described in Chapter 2. Six-pound-test line is sufficient and the bobber should be no larger than a dime. For most types of live baits intended for bluegills, I suggest a size 10 long-shanked hook. Since bluegills have small mouths, and customarily inhale live baits very deeply, a long-shanked hook can more easily be extracted than a short-shanked hook.

The most popular bait is a small catalpa or garden worm. But other anglers prefer crickets, grasshoppers, or freshwater shrimp, either in their live form or those which have been preserved by freeze-drying and which can quickly be reconstituted by adding water to their packages.

The method of presenting any of these baits with a long panfish pole is easy to learn. From a standing position, merely extend the rod as far as you can reach and gently set the bait down so that when it sinks it is suspended beneath the float about one foot above the spawning bed.

One thing that is vitally important, however, is positioning the boat in such a manner that you work the outside perimeter of the clustered beds first, as this enables you to hook and land a large number of fish without unduly disturbing the others in the central part of the bedding area. After the outside perimeter has been thoroughly worked, move in several yards closer and work the interior of the bedding grounds.

Using a long fiberglass or graphite panfish pole is most effective when the water is slightly dingy colored and retards visibility. If the water is ultra-clear, however, it may be difficult to approach a colonial nesting ground to within reach of the pole's length without alarming the fish and having them quickly scoot away. Now is when lightweight spinning tackle should be considered, so the bait can be presented from a cautious distance.

A 5-foot ultralight rod, with either an

open- or closed-faced reel, is fine, with the recommended terminal rigging being the same as with a panfish pole.

Although live bait is lethal for spring bluegills, using a fly rod and an assortment of artificials is, in my opinion, far more fun. It is also entirely hassle-free, as one can well imagine when contemplating the possibility of catching perhaps fifty or more bluegills over the course of several hours and having to re-bait that many hooks.

An adequate fly rod for bluegilling can be a relatively inexpensive model of hollow-fiberglass construction. In order that these feisty battlers can give their best showing, however, I recommend a rod no more than 7 feet in length with a very light tip action.

My favorite is an ultralight rod only 6 feet in length weighing a feathery 1.5 ounces! When I'm lucky enough to hook a "pounder" with this little beauty, it bends into an inverted U and the fish invariably makes several runs and may even jump clear of the water two or three times.

Incidentally, on behalf of youngsters or adult beginners who wish to use artificials but are not well-practiced with fly tackle, there is an acceptable alternative. It is the clear plastic bubble, used in conjunction with lightweight spinning tackle.

A clear plastic bubble somewhat resembles a small bobber and it attaches to the line in the same manner, thus affording casting weight with light offerings such as flies and poppers tied to the terminal end of the line. If you select a traditional floating lure such as a dry fly or tiny popper, simply attach the bobber two feet above the lure and begin casting. You can also fish intermediate depths, and still deeper water, by holding the bobber beneath the surface, turning a tiny dial, and allowing the bobber to fill with any desired amount of water, depending upon the depth of the spawning beds in question.

SUMMER AND FALL BLUEGILLS

When spawning is completed, bluegills begin drifting into deeper water. If the particular cove, embayment, or wide creek arm they spawned in has water depths to twelve feet or more, the fish may remain right there for the remainder of the year. But if such depths do

When fishing from shore where flycasting would be difficult, floating flies, bugs, and poppers can nevertheless be cast with spinning tackle and a clear plastic bubble.

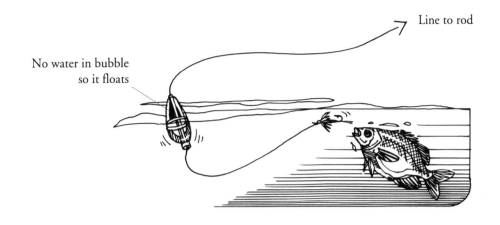

No water in bubble
so it floats

Line to rod

Line to rod

Bobber partly filled
with water so it sinks

Lake floor

Plastic bubble can also be partly filled with water for fishing deeper when bluegills are not feeding on the surface.

not exist, the fish will predictably move toward the main lake basin.

In either case—whether the fish stay in the bay and creeks where they spawned or move to the main lake proper—there is a single word that describes where they'll be. That word is edge.

In other words, bluegills (and all other sunfish, as well) have a distinct preference for the interface where two different types of cover or structure meet. The most common type of edge where bluegills congregate is a weedline where the water depth drops off abruptly; the particular species of weeds most frequently used by bluegills include bulrushes, cattails,

reeds, sawgrass, eel grass, lily pads, cabomba, milfoil, hyacinth, cabbage, and coontail.

In the North, where weeds are not as prevalent as in more southerly latitudes, bluegills show an affinity for jumbled rock formations and gravel reefs on the bottom. Yet still again, it's the edges around the circumference of such bottom structures, where the rocky cover yields to a sandy or muddy bottom composition, that seem to hold the most fish, rather than the central portions of the rocky cover.

Bluegills adhere to many other types of edges, too, such as the stump-littered lips of inundated stream and creek channels on the bottom that wind their way through embayments toward the main lake basin. Also, along the shoreline of the main lake proper, an underwater shelf typically extends outward various distances before suddenly dropping into very deep water. The edge which exists there, especially if it has scattered brush, often attracts very large bluegills, particularly in late summer.

An aisle of thick-standing timber separating a swamp from the open water of the main lake likewise constitutes an edge, and points of land which extend into the lake underwater before dropping off steeply at their tip ends are edges.

Shoreline trees which have toppled into the water are also types of edges because they disrupt the continuity of the bank. The most productive trees are conifers, oaks, and willows because they have a dense latticework of

When spawning is completed, larger bluegills vacate the shorelines but remain in relatively shallow water in a lake's feeder tributaries and large embayments where there's plenty of cover.

branches that afford more hiding places than other species. Moreover, when any type of cover is found in conjunction with a marked change in the bottom contour of the lake it will attract far more fish. In other words, if a tree falls into the water along an otherwise featureless shoreline where the bottom composition is smooth and gently tapering, it will undoubtedly attract some bluegills; but not nearly as many as a fallen tree by a drop-off or along a rubble-strewn shoreline.

During the summer and fall, manmade structures also attract bluegills in great numbers. Anglers frequently gather discarded Christmas trees at the end of the holiday season, drag them onto the frozen ice of lakes, and tie a concrete block to the tree for weight. When the ice melts in spring, the tree sinks right there, and if the angler has wisely marked its location on a map he can be assured of catching bluegills there the following summer.

Other manmade features that attract bluegills in modest numbers include boat docks, marinas, piers, jetties, railway trestles, bridge abutments, causeways, and even duck blinds.

Throughout the summer and fall, bluegills are not nearly as depth-conscious as some other panfish species such as yellow perch. Generally most of the larger fish may find cover at depths ranging from three to twenty feet. I usually start fishing at a weedline edge near a former spawning area, if the water there is at least six to eight feet deep. If there are no well-defined weedline edges in close proximity to the former spawning grounds, I'll look instead for scattered rock piles on the bottom, or a meandering creek channel, using a depth sounder and contour map if I'm not intimately familiar with the water. Passing weeks will then invariably see me slowly moving in the direction of the main lake basin, fishing ever-deeper weedline edges bordering open water, deep rock piles and gravel reefs, and investigating shoreline drop-offs, deep stump beds and the like.

TACKLE TECHNIQUES

We've devoted a good deal of time to fish location through the seasons because, when it comes to panfishing, and bluegills and sunfish in particular, I've always believed that finding the fish is the most important consideration. Once that has been accomplished, there are a wide variety of lures and fishing methods that can be employed to catch the critters.

When test-fishing various areas where the water depth does not exceed ten feet, the very same rods, reels, lures, and live baits described in the spawning section can be put into play with only minor refinements.

For example, the angler who elects to fish with live bait, using a 14-foot telescoping panfish pole, will want to adjust his bobber accordingly to work all levels in two-foot increments right down to the bottom.

The fly fisherman will undoubtedly want to cast surface-riding dry flies and foam-bodied bugs at first, just as when fishing spawning beds, yet he is advised to have a second fly rod rigged up (or, at least, a second reel) with a sinking-tip line to work nymphs and wet flies at deeper levels.

And the spin fisherman who elects to cast live baits will want to use a slip-bobber rig, which is described in detail in Chapter 2. Similarly, if the spin fisherman prefers to cast assorted insect imitations, he'll want to use a clear plastic bubble for casting weight and remember to periodically add more water to the bubble to take it and his offering to deeper levels.

But now let's look at still other types of situations, and tackle techniques, in which bluegills may be caught during summer and fall.

In going back to the bluegill's preference for weeds, and more specifically the edges of weeds, one of the most lethal methods is to create your own private, temporary fishing holes. Simply find an area where there is extensive, heavily matted weed growth floating on the surface.

Then, create several pothole openings or channels far back in the weeds.

Some anglers accomplish this by using a common garden rake that can be fitted with a six-foot extension of lightweight aluminum tubing. Next, ease your boat in tight against the edge of the thick vegetation, reach out the approximate twelve-foot length of the rake and scoop out a hole about four feet in diameter in the matted weeds. Then, move thirty or forty yards farther down the weedline and create another pothole beyond the leading edge.

An alternative to using a garden rake to create openings is simply running your outboard through the weeds to create a long, winding channel.

After you've created perhaps eight potholes, or a long channel, return to your starting point and begin casting floating bugs, poppers, or flies. Or, if you have a long panfish pole, reach out and dabble live baits. Or use spinning tackle to cast a live bait suspended just slightly beneath a bobber.

In any case, be prepared for fast action! During the dog days of mid to late summer, bluegills and sunfish like to swim far back beneath a canopy of matted vegetation where the water temperature is cooler and there is respite from the bright sunlight. Therefore, when a pothole or channel suddenly is created, it's like ringing a dinner bell to the seemingly always-hungry panfish. Countless insects, scuds, and other aquatic lifeforms are dislodged during the creation of the hole or channel and bluegills will gravitate toward the opening.

Another dynamite tactic few anglers are familiar with can be used when bluegills are near the shoreline in water ten to twenty-five feet deep. This is vertically jigging with an ice-fishing rod. I know, it sounds preposterous, and that may be precisely why only a small coterie of very accomplished anglers use the technique.

The ice-fishing rod can be a commercially made model, or simply the tip section of a bro-

Throughout the summer, bluegills congregate in and around heavy cover, especially vegetation. When weed growth becomes heavily matted on the surface during late summer, make channels by running your outboard through the weeds, then return to fish the created edges.

ken fly or spinning rod inserted into a section of wooden dowel. Tape an ultralight spinning reel to the handle, or a fly reel spooled with 6-pound test mono. For greater sensitivity than the tip of the rod itself can afford, most anglers fabricate a short tip extension made from lightweight wire, with the end bent into a circle to serve as the tip guide.

As to the lures themselves, small jigs are the order of the day. In fact, some manufacturers refer to these particular panfish offerings as micro jigs because they range in weight from $\frac{1}{32}$ to $\frac{1}{100}$ of an ounce.

These jigs come in a wide variety of nondescript designs, some in traditional round-head ball design, others which are more elongated in shape, with various types of plastic tails and in numerous color combinations. You can even use so-called ice flies, which are teardrop-shaped metal jigs primarily designed for ice fishing and described in Chapter 14.

In any event, as we said earlier, baitfish and minnows comprise only a small fraction of a bluegill's diet. They are primarily insect feeders and are not inclined to chase after fast-moving food of any type. Consequently, allow the jig to sink to the bottom directly beneath the boat and swim it very s-l-o-w-l-y by just barely moving your rod tip from side to side.

Better still, I've found, is to select jigs that vaguely represent grubs, larval, or insect forms and fish them by simply jiggling them in place

As fall approaches, and the water cools, bluegills move into the depths. Catch them now by vertically jigging tandem wet flies or jigs.

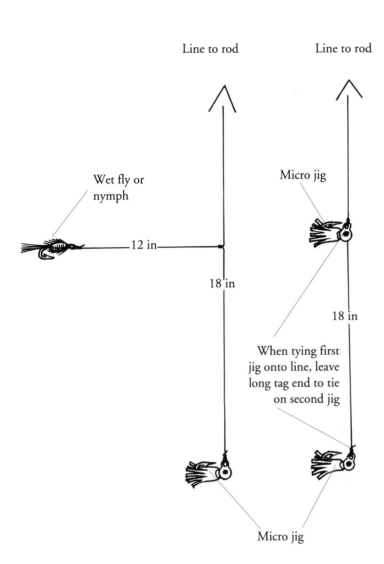

Line to rod

Line to rod

Wet fly or nymph

Micro jig

—12 in—

18 in

18 in

When tying first jig onto line, leave long tag end to tie on second jig

Micro jig

with long pauses in between each movement of the lure. Moreover, you can greatly enhance your catch rate if you "sweeten" the lure with a maggot, mealworm, or wax worm impaled on the hook.

Many anglers even fish two lures simultaneously in an attempt to determine what the panfish want on a given day. They'll tie a micro jig to the end of the line and a wet fly or nymph of a different color to a dropper tied into the line about 18 inches above.

Finally, since bluegills and sunfish are aggressive feeders and, once located, are relatively easy to catch by a variety of means, don't dilly-dally in one place. If you've spent fifteen minutes working a stumpy bottom area at the edge of deep water with no results, move to another location and then still another. Eventually you'll strike paydirt.

5

Six Favorite Sunfish

Some anglers claim that trout are the most strikingly beautiful freshwater fish. Maybe, but the riotously hued sunfish clan will give them stiff competition. In fact, some anglers even contend the "sunfish" moniker is in specific reference to the bright yellows, oranges, and reds that typify the body colorations of most of the sunfishes. But biologists maintain that the name refers to their penchant for basking in warm, brightly illuminated shallows.

In any event, there are at least twenty-five known sunfish species inhabiting the North American continent, of which the bluegill is by far the most popular. That's why we devoted the entire previous chapter to the bluegill.

Here we'll take a brief look at still other members of the sunfish tribe, but not all of them, as many do not grow larger than two or three inches and thus are not pursued by anglers.

That brings us to the redear sunfish, pumpkinseed, redbreast sunfish, green sunfish, longear sunfish, and warmouth. Aside from the bluegill, they are my six favorite sunfishes because each has a relatively wide distribution, all provide a sporting account of themselves when

caught with appropriate tackle, and each deserves a very high rating on the dinner table.

At the outset, it should be mentioned that nearly all of the fishing techniques, tackle, live baits, and artificial lures described in the previous chapter on bluegills apply to the sunfishes discussed here. Indeed, as noted in the previous chapter, when two or more sunfish species inhabit the same body of water they commonly hybridize, which not only sometimes makes precise species identification difficult but results in a good deal of similarity in their behavior. In fact, on many occasions around the country, I've caught, on consecutive casts, alternately a bluegill, a pumpkinseed, and a green sunfish from the same location on the same lure or bait. Then, on the very next cast, I've landed another sunfish of entirely unknown parentage.

Nevertheless, it is important to look at each of the other popular sunfish species because occasionally there are subtle ways in which they differ from bluegills in terms of their habitat and food preferences. And sometimes these differences translate into slightly different methods of catching them.

Because they hybridize, the various sunfishes sometimes defy proper identification, but there are subtle differences in coloration and body shape that provide clues.

The redear is our largest sunfish. Just one monster like this can provide a meal for two!

A splendid example of how a working knowledge of catching bluegills can, with only minor changes in technique, be directly applied to catching another panfish species is the case of the redear sunfish.

REDEAR

The redear often lives side by side with bluegills, sharing the same habitat and forage base. Yet unlike any of the other sunfishes, the redear has a fetish for snails, small crayfish and tiny mollusks and will grab them at any opportunity. Nature has even given the species a unique set of grinding teeth in the back of its mouth which are specifically designed for crushing shells. Thus, it is not strange that around the country the redear sunfish's most common nickname is the *shellcracker,* and anglers who target the species commonly rely upon small brown or black jigs that resemble the redear's favorite food.

The original range of the redear sunfish, *Lep-*

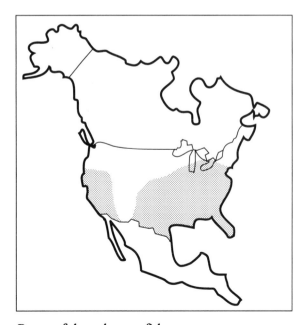

Range of the redear sunfish.

omis microlophus, was the deep South, stretching from Texas to Florida and north into the Carolinas. But transplanting efforts have long since enlarged the redear's range all the way to the Great Lakes, throughout the Midwest, and even into select regions of the desert Southwest.

Redear sunfish thrive in the very same types of lakes, reservoirs, rivers, and ponds inhabited by bluegills. But keep the following differences in mind: throughout the year, redears customarily prefer slightly deeper water than bluegills and, although they like weeds, have a special fondness for brush, logs and stumps.

The redear's name tells all. Its most identifying characteristic is a red fringe surrounding the rearmost tip of the male's black ear flap; the female's black ear flap is margined with orange, and in males and females alike the very outermost edges may have a white strip beyond the red or orange border. In certain waters, the shellcracker's body coloration may closely resemble that of the pumpkinseed but is readily distinguished because the redear does not sport wavy blue lines on its cheeks, as does the pumpkinseed. Otherwise, the redear's body coloration is dark golden along the dorsal region, blending into silvery-green along the sides and yellow on the belly. During the breeding period, males often turn so dark in color they appear almost solid black, which is believed to excite female redears into dropping their eggs.

The redear, by far, achieves the largest average size of any of the sunfish species. The world record, from Virginia, weighed 4 pounds, and 1-pound shellcrackers a full 12 inches in length are as common as ¾-pound bluegills.

Redear sunfish spawn in the same types of areas as bluegills, yet they often are easier to locate because their colonies are much larger. Sometimes the beds number in the hundreds and in select regions, usually in the deep South, the renowned, action-packed fishing afforded by spawning shellcrackers gives birth to fishing festivals and derbies, with local shops and busi-

Redear sunfish are easily located during the spring by bubbles on the surface over their spawning beds.

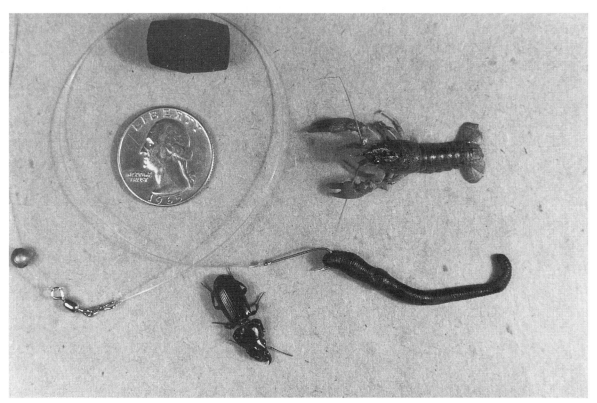

Redears are nicknamed "shellcrackers" because they feed heavily upon snails, crayfish, and crickets. But worms and artificials such as jigs also are effective. Note the slip-shot sinker which takes the bait down and the black foam bobber which keeps the offering slightly off the bottom where redears usually feed.

nesses even closing down as for any celebrated holiday. It is not unusual for a bedding area to be so large, in fact, that it may accommodate several boats simultaneously with perhaps half a dozen anglers accounting for more than a thousand fish in a single afternoon.

Bedding areas, being so large, can be readily identified by simply motoring around in shallow areas. Also watch for bubbles on the surface. Redears are more energetic in their nest building activities than bluegills and their vigorous fanning out of beds with their tails often causes countless bubbles to speckle the surface.

Although anglers can catch redear sunfish with precisely the same live baits also selected for bluegill fishing, the most effective ones are crickets, crayfish, or perhaps a small nightcrawler hooked just once through the nose. When using a telescoping panfish pole and bobber, or light spinning tackle, be sure to adjust your float so the bait touches bottom, or very near to it, because the shellcracker is primarily a bottom forager.

Since redear sunfish generally like to "mouth" their prey rather than inhaling it all at once, I often use a slip-shot (a split-shot with a hole through the center). This enables a fish to take the bait without feeling resistance. Moreover, I don't attempt to set the hook until I see the line begin to tighten, or move sideways, indicating the shellcracker has the bait fully inside his mouth and is beginning to move away with it.

Artificial lures, primarily jigs or dark-colored nymphs, should likewise be fished near the bottom, either by slowly retrieving them or working them suspended below a small bobber, as described in detail in Chapter 2.

At the conclusion of their spawning activities, shellcrackers scatter widely, retreating into water where the depth may range from ten to twenty-five feet. Look for them near deep weedlines, drop-offs, deep rock piles, ledge outcroppings, and the edges of inundated stream channels on the lake floor. Keep in mind that any such locations which have brush, logs, or stumps present are more attractive to redears. The recommended tackle for catching redears under these conditions consists of live baits or jigs fished with slip-bobber rigs (as described in Chapter 2). Yet since the fish now, and for the remainder of the year, are congregating only in loose numbers, and therefore do not customarily afford the fast action and heavy stringers associated with the spawning season, many anglers turn their attention to other species.

Pumpkinseed sunfish sport bright, eclectic colors but seldom grow very large. The world record was only 12 ounces.

PUMPKINSEED

Pumpkinseeds are unquestionably the most stunning of all the panfish species. They display a wide array of bright, iridescent colors, with sides a dappled patchwork of gold, yellow, and red specks on a pale green background, an almost neon-like emerald or blue glow to the edges of the tail and dorsal fins, wavy blue lines accentuating the cheeks, and red or orange crescents adorning its gill flaps. It is impossible to mistake the pumpkinseed for any other sunfish.

Known to biologists as *Lepomis gibbosus*, the pumpkinseed was originally distributed throughout the upper Midwest and along the eastern seaboard. Yet the species has since found its way into the deep South and across the upper Northwest. In many locales, anglers refer to pumpkinseeds as *tobacco boxes, pond perch, sunnies, red bellies, or robins.*

An average adult pumpkinseed is about the same size as an average bluegill, meaning 7 inches in length and perhaps one-half pound in weight. Yet even in protected environments where pumpkinseeds are able to live many years, they seldom grow much larger. By comparison, the world-record bluegill exceeded 4 pounds, yet the world-record pumpkinseed, which was taken in South Dakota in 1970,

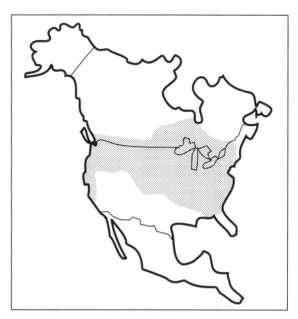

Range of the pumpkinseed sunfish.

tipped the scales at a mere 12-ounces.

The pumpkinseed's preferred habitat makes him an easy target for anglers, for the species does best in small, quiet, shallow, weedy lakes and ponds. When fishing in the largest man-made reservoirs, forget about the wide expanses of open mid-lake areas, which pumpkinseeds rarely inhabit, and search for shallow, protected bays, coves, and creek arms where the species

Pumpkinseeds spend the entire year in very shallow water. Look for them in coves, creek arms, and protected coves where the water remains calm.

predictably spends the entire year.

Spring spawning behavior of the pumpkinseed is identical to that of the bluegill, with the exception that pumpkinseeds quite often are found closer to the banks and in water only six inches deep. When spawning is concluded, they spend the remaining months of the year in and around weedy cover, seldom venturing deeper than five or six feet.

Since pumpkinseeds feed heavily upon insects, the fly-rodder armed with a selection of flies, bugs, and nymphs can enjoy fast action throughout the summer. However, since pumpkinseeds, like redear sunfish, also dote upon invertebrates such as snails, and have a similar set of coarse teeth in their throats for crushing shells, tiny jigs weighing no more than ⅛ ounce are likewise ideal lures for the species. Small garden worms, crickets, insect larva such as mealworms or waxworms are the best live baits.

Whether you fish artificial lures or live bait, keep in mind that pumpkinseeds have somewhat smaller mouths than the other sunfish, so use small lures with hooks no larger than size 10 or size 8 hooks with live baits.

REDBREAST

The redbreast is another vibrantly hued species with a host of regional nicknames. Biologists know the fish as *Lepomis auritus,* but if you hear anyone referring to *yellow-bellies, yellowbreasts,*

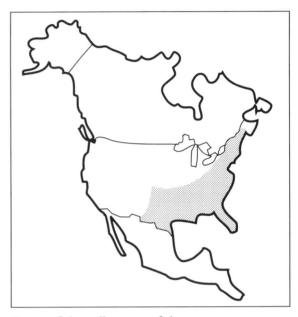

Range of the redbreast sunfish.

The redbreast sunfish is such an aggressive feeder that most anglers don't waste time using live baits but rely upon a wide variety of artificial lures.

robbins, or *robbinperch* they are undoubtedly talking about redbreast sunfish.

Originally, the redbreast was native to those streams and rivers in the southeastern states that flowed into the Atlantic. Today, however, the species inhabits all of the eastern seaboard states and most of the south-central states. Although redbreasts make their homes in a wide variety of lakes and reservoirs, they seem to do even better in moderately clear rivers and streams.

Redbreasts do not achieve large sizes, with adult fish seldom exceeding ¾ pound in weight and 9 inches in length, but they are spirited fighters and delicious table fare. The world-record redbreast, caught in South Carolina in 1975, weighed 2 pounds.

In appearance the redbreast certainly lives up to its name. Its ventral region is a striking red or orange-yellow, which makes it difficult to confuse the species with any other. Its sides generally are olive-brown or golden, sometimes accentuated with dark vertical bars and bright red flecks. As with the pumpkinseed, bright blue lines can usually be seen radiating from the mouth back over the gill plates; yet unlike the pumpkinseed the redbreast has a long, narrow, dark gill flap.

Redbreasts spawn under the same conditions as the other sunfishes, although they seem more tolerant of muddy-bottomed bays, coves, and creek arms. Moreover, redbreasts are not colonial spawners like bluegills and redear sunfish but tend instead to build solitary nests, often against logs or the exposed root masses of stumps and standing trees.

When spawning is concluded, redbreasts head for deep weedbeds and the edges of weed-lines that rapidly give way to deep water. Fish these types of water anywhere you find them—in isolated deep coves or along main-lake shore-lines—and finding redbreasts should not be difficult.

The redbreast sunfish is popular with anglers because of its aggressive feeding behavior. It will hit a wide variety of artificial lures worked along the bottom, across the surface, or anywhere in between. This means virtually any type of fly-rod panfish lure is an acceptable choice, including surface poppers and dry flies, wet flies and nymphs, foam-bodied bugs, and similar insect imitations. Compared to the other sunfishes, the redbreast feeds avidly after dark, so a prime time to be on the water is late evening.

It also is important to mention that, compared to several of the other sunfish species, the redbreast has a somewhat larger mouth and eagerly feeds upon minnows as well. Consequently, straight-shaft spinners account for their share of fish, as do small crappie jigs dressed with curlytail grubs, and inch-long streamer flies. Of course, spinning tackle is customarily used to cast spinners and jigs, but streamers and other flies can also be used by the spin-fisherman by simply attaching a clear plastic bubble to the line.

In the live bait category, any offering that appeals to bluegills and the other sunfishes is likewise a good choice for redbreasts as well. However, if you can find them, or live-trap them yourself, small pin minnows, no more than an inch in length, are the best bet.

GREEN SUNFISH

The green sunfish inhabits an extensive portion of North America. Other than New England, the highest elevations of the Rocky Mountain states, and the extreme northwest, *Lepomis cyanellus* is found in every state.

Undoubtedly, it's the expansive border-to-border, coast-to-coast range of the green sunfish that explains why this particular species is the one that most frequently hybridizes with the bluegill. Known regionally as the *blue-spotted sunnie, green perch,* or *black perch,* the green sunfish has a penchant for interbreeding with bluegills that frequently makes it difficult to

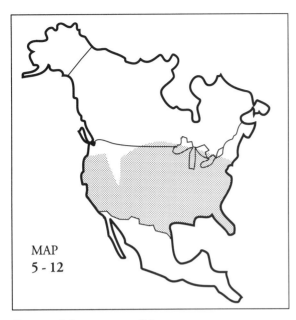

MAP
5 - 12

Range of the green sunfish.

positively identify the species by coloration and body markings alone.

As one might expect, the green sunfish's body is basically green, with emerald and yellow reflections that gradually blend into yellow along the ventral region. The cheeks have prominent blue streaks and the ear flap is short and black, with an amber- colored fringe around the margin. For undisputed identification, keep in mind that a pure strain green sunfish has short,

rounded pectoral fins whereas the bluegill has long, pointed pectorals. But the most noticeable difference is the mouth, with that of the green sunfish being quite oversize by comparison, having heavy lips and closely resembling that of a rock bass. Whenever green sunfish and bluegills hybridize, the offspring are a curious looking combination of the two.

Green sunfish are the most hardy of the sunfish clan, which enables them to do just fine in bodies of water their close cousins could not tolerate. Of course, they are found living under the best water-quality conditions. But don't discount a lake, reservoir, or river from consideration simply because it is known to be excessively turbid, low in dissolved oxygen content, or which experiences radical fluctuations in water temperature or pool level, because chances are the green sunfish will be the predominant panfish species in that particular body of water.

One tip worth mentioning is to avoid farm ponds. Green sunfish are so prolific that they can rapidly decimate other fish populations in small bodies of water by consuming all of the available food and then raiding the spawning nests of other panfish and gamefish species. Consequently, landowners usually keep green sunfish out of such waters. Wherever the species does appear, the individuals are likely to be stunted.

Adult green sunfish seldom exceed 8 inches

The green sunfish is the one that most commonly interbreeds with other species. It also is more tolerant of turbid, muddy, or stagnant water.

Green sunfish live out their entire lives in home areas less than a half acre in size. They especially like quiet backwater regions choked with brush.

in length and ½ pound in weight. A brace of identical 2-pound, 2-ounce fish share the world-record slot, one from Kansas and the other from Missouri.

Green sunfish are generally homebodies. In the spring they filter into shallow, narrow creek arms to spawn. But shortly thereafter, once mating is completed, they typically drift only short distances away to spend the remainder of the year in slightly deeper portions of that particular creek arm or an adjacent connecting cove or embayment. Although the species likes to hang around the fringes of weedbeds, it distinctly prefers jumbled boulders and rock formations on the bottom, felled trees, drowned brush, and stump beds.

Green sunfish engage in their most active feeding behavior at dawn and dusk. Owing to their comparatively large mouths, they commonly forage upon foods that would be too large for the other sunfish species. Bait fishermen do well with small crayfish, crickets, grasshoppers, earthworms, and minnows up to 2 inches in length. Yet since green sunfish are

opportunists, it stands to reason the fly or spin-fisherman can enjoy equally fast action with a variety of flies, bugs, and poppers that resemble insects, as well as ⅛-ounce jigs dressed with plastic tails and even spinner-fly combinations.

LONGEAR SUNFISH

As its name suggests, the longear sunfish is easy to identify by its unusually long ear flap, which is dark and trimmed with a thin border of red or yellow. The back, sides, and belly are a combination of blue-green, emerald, and orange hues accentuated by brilliant blue streaks, making it a beautiful fish indeed. The pectoral fins are rounded and short.

Its official moniker is *Lepomis megalotis,* but anglers commonly refer to the species as the *big-eared sunfish, red-bellied bream, blackeared sunfish,* or *red-eyed sunfish* (because of its red iris).

The longear's range encompasses all of the south central states as well as those stretching up

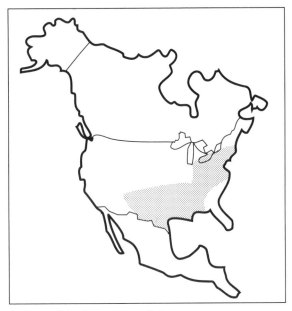

Range of the longear sunfish.

largest known specimen, caught in New Mexico in 1979, didn't even weigh a full pound.

Longears prefer quiet, shallow, backwater areas of coves, embayments, and creek arms and even during the warmest midsummer months rarely venture deeper than six feet. Their spawning habits are identical to those of the bluegill, and when mating is concluded they seem to prefer weedy cover to rocks or brush.

Although longear sunfish are voracious feeders, they spook quite easily when their immediate area is disturbed, so maintain a cautious casting distance. For this reason, even the longest panfish poles often prove too short, a paradox that nearly always results in fly rods or spinning rods getting the nod.

Moreover, because of the longear's diminutive size, artificial lures should be quite small. Since the longear's diet is comprised mainly of insects, the angler's assortment of dry flies, wet flies, nymphs, and foam-bodied bugs should be tied on size 12 hooks or smaller. In the live bait category, larvae such as maggots, waxworms, mealworms, freshwater shrimp, small crickets, and earthworms are the best choices.

the Mississippi drainage system into Ohio, Pennsylvania, and several of the Atlantic coastal states. Although the longear sunfish is widely distributed and provides good sport, alas, it seldom reaches impressive size. Adult fish seldom exceed 7 inches or 10 ounces in weight. The

The longear sunfish sports a distinctive large earflap and commonly interbreeds with green sunfish. Thus it seldom exceeds 8 inches.

WARMOUTH

The final member of my selection of six favorite sunfish is *Lepomis gulosus*, which anglers sometimes refer to as the goggleye or warmouth bass. Quite frequently, this particular species is confused with the rock bass. Since both fish look nearly identical, many anglers never learn to tell the difference between them, but there are ways to ensure proper identification.

First, the warmouth's anal fin has three spines, whereas that of the rock bass has six. Also, although the warmouth has a relatively large mouth that is similar to that of the rock bass, the species has rough teeth on its tongue, a feature that is absent in the rock bass. The warmouth also has several brown streaks flaring back from its mouth and across its gill covers.

As for its body coloration, the warmouth sports the same olive brown hue as the rock bass, along with dark mottled splotches, and a ventral region that is dark amber. Yet in many waters the warmouth also displays glistening flecks of violet and gold on its sides.

The species is well distributed throughout the eastern, southeastern, south-central, and southwestern states. It usually inhabits shallow, muddy-bottomed lakes, reservoirs, sloughs, and swamps. Water that is slightly stagnant is tolerated by this hardy species. Of all the sunfish species, the warmouth is the strongest in

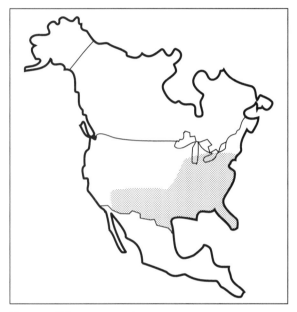

Range of the warmouth.

Look for warmouths inhabiting muddy waters, especially in swamps and sloughs where there is brush cover. The species feeds heavily at dawn, then becomes relatively inactive for the remainder of the day.

its partiality for heavy cover in the form of weeds, felled trees, brush, logs, stumps and, preferably, a combination of all.

The warmouth does not grow to appreciable size. A 10-inch fish weighing a pound is considered a large one, with the world record, taken in South Carolina in 1973, being slightly more than 2 pounds.

Interestingly, the warmouth is primarily an early morning feeder and frequently disdains even the most delectable food item once the sun has fully cleared the horizon. Keep this in mind if the warmouth is the target of your next outing.

When the fish do indeed feed, they can be coaxed into taking virtually any offering that resembles insect life, larval forms, small minnows, or small crayfish.

The spawning habits of warmouths are the same as bluegills and, like green sunfish, they live out their entire lives in relatively small areas. Therefore, look for them in typical sunfish spawning habitat in the spring and for the remainder of the year associating with the heaviest cover in the same immediate area.

6

All About Crappies

Legions of anglers call crappies Public Panfish No. 1, and the reasons are obvious.

For one, crappies can be caught year-round, even when winter ice blankets lakes and reservoirs. The fish also are relatively easy to locate. This means you can count on fast action even on an unfamiliar lake or whenever the fishing for other panfish species is slow. Moreover, the fish are prized for their flavor, and an angler can fill his freezer with crappies without fear of decimating the population because few states impose size or creel limits. In fact, the species are so prolific and have such a tendency to overpopulate their habitat that biologists recommend keeping all you catch. Finally, sophisticated tackle is not required to dupe crappies.

When you tally up the score, few other fish species, anywhere, provide so much for such a widely varied cross-section of anglers.

GETTING TO KNOW CRAPPIES

Actually, there are two species of crappies and they are so nearly identical that many anglers have difficulty telling them apart. There is the

Crappies are excellent table fare, and they reproduce in such large numbers that anglers can make huge catches with little danger to the population.

The white crappie is usually (not always) lighter hued than the black crappie. For positive identification, count the stiff spines of the dorsal fin.

The black crappie usually (not always) has a dark, speckled coloration and seven or eight spines on the dorsal fin.

white crappie, *Pomoxis annularis,* and the black crappie, *Pomoxis nigro-maculatus.* Both tend to have a silvery-greenish color, but the white crappie sports vertical, dark bands while the black crappie has a dappled array of dark splotches. Yet the particular water chemistry of a given lake can cause any fish species to take on slightly lighter or darker hues than otherwise, so color alone is not always an accurate means of distinguishing between the two crappies. To be absolutely sure, count the stiff spines of the dorsal fin. If the count is six, it's a white crappie. If it's seven or eight, it's a black crappie.

Interestingly, crappies have a host of colorful nicknames, depending upon the region of the country. Throughout the South, the name is pronounced just as it is spelled. But north of the Mason-Dixon line, the name is pronounced "croppie." In various locales, they also are referred to as *specks, papermouths, silversides, bachelor perch, speckled perch, chinquapin,* and *lamplighters.* Still other monikers include *strawberry bass, calico bass, white perch, banlicks, tinmouths,* and *sac-a-lait* (Cajun-French for "bag of milk," in reference to their succulent white flesh).

White and black crappies are members of the sunfish family and their original range, included all states east of the Mississippi with the exception of New England and Florida. However, transplanting efforts going back as far as seventy-five years ago have long since expanded that range across the Midwest and to the Pacific coast states as well. Today, the only regions which do not possess high crappie populations are the

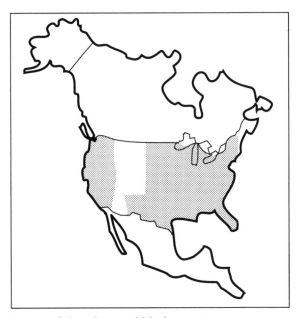

Range of the white and black crappie.

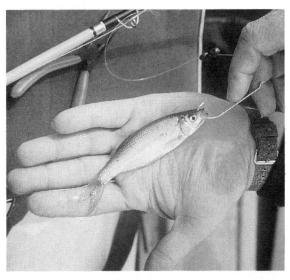

Although both species of crappies are opportunists when it comes to feeding, their all-time favorites are minnows of various species.

Rocky Mountain states, New England, and southern Florida.

Today, neither the black crappie nor the white crappie has its own exclusive habitat. Originally, black crappies were more abundant in cooler, deeper, clearer waters possessing sand/gravel bottoms, and they favored rocky structure and weedy cover. Conversely, white crappies were more prevalent in warmer, shallower, turbid, soft-bottomed waters, and they preferred standing timber and brush cover. But that rule of thumb no longer holds true. Today, north or south, east or west, the two species may inhabit the very same waters in great abundance and an angler fishing a piece of cover in a given lake may alternately catch one species and then the other.

Like all panfish, white and black crappies are opportunists when it comes to feeding. Their favorite forage consists of small minnow species averaging 1 to 4 inches in length. As a result, live minnows are universally the most popular bait. But crappies also eat upon the young fry and fingerlings of other panfish, crustaceans such as small crayfish and snails, mollusks, tadpoles, and a variety of insects. Although the two species can be caught at any hour, they are more light-sensitive than other panfishes. Therefore, the prime times to catch them are at dawn, dusk, and especially after full dark.

A majority of crappies average 7 to 10 inches in length and weigh ½ to ¾ pound, but 12- to 16-inch fish weighing 2 to 3 pounds (which are referred to as *slabs*) are quite common. The world-record white crappie, from Mississippi, weighed slightly more than 5 pounds and the world-record black crappie, weighing 6 pounds, had Louisiana water dripping from its gills.

CRAPPIES THROUGH THE SEASONS

In the spring, when the water temperature reaches 55 degrees, enormous schools of crappies invade shallow water to spawn. This is unquestionably when the largest catches are made.

Most spawning takes place at depths of three

During the spring spawning period, look for crappies in shallow bays and creek arms containing drowned brush and treetops.

to seven feet, but the nests are not as well fanned out as those made by other sunfishes and are not very visible. "Blind fishing" many spots may be required to find the fish. Happily, however, once an angler has caught a couple of crappies he can be fairly confident numerous others are in the immediate vicinity.

As the season progresses, white crappies and black crappies engage in the type of classic migrations that are quite typical of largemouth bass. That is, in early spring they move out of deep water and begin gathering at the mouths of creek arms and the entrances to shallow embayments. Then, when some cosmic signal urges them on, they move progressively shallower, following bottom contours such as drop-offs or stream channels on the floor, far back into the creek arms and embayments. Actual spawning generally takes place in the back half of the feeder tributary arm, or shallow flats of the bay, where there is drowned brush, tree tops, bushes, and similar woody cover on the bottom. In the absence of woody cover, look for the first signs of emerging weed growth. When spawning is completed, the fish then begin their well-planned journey back to deeper water, entirely abandoning all but the deepest coves and creek arms for main lake areas. By midsummer, they usually can be found near stump fields and standing timber on deep shoreline drop-offs or

Unlike the various sunfish species, crappies do not fan out well-defined spawning beds but merely bump their ventral regions on bottom debris to release their eggs and milt.

Small, slim punt boats are popular with crappie anglers because they can be precisely maneuvered in and around irregular shaped cover.

Throughout the spring, a simple yet highly effective way to catch crappies is with a stand-up bobber and either a tiny jig or hook baited with a live minnow.

along the edges of an old riverbed winding across the lake floor. In winter the fish congregate in deep holes or the riverbed proper.

TWO DEADLY SPRING-FISHING METHODS

Lakes which have reputations as crappie hotspots commonly see a flotilla of "punt boats" on the water in early spring. These are tiny affairs, typically no more than 6 feet in length, often with a freeboard of no more than a foot. They're one-man jobs, powered by an electric motor or sculling paddle, and they often appear as though they might be in danger of swamping. Actually, however, there is little danger because use of the shallow-draft boats is restricted to calm backwaters where the depth generally is less than five feet.

Although any lightweight johnboat or aluminum V-bottom can be used for spring crappie fishing, punt boats are specifically designed for the undertaking because they are narrow and can be adroitly maneuvered around brush piles and "wiggled" into tiny places with a minimum of effort.

No matter which type of boat you use, the method of catching the fish is fairly well standardized. The venerable cane pole is simple, inexpensive, and efficient. But most veteran crappie anglers use a long fiberglass or graphite panfish pole. Most are telescopic for easy transportation and then, on the water, extend to 12 or even 16 feet in length. A reel is not necessary, but if one is mounted on the rod it invariably is an inexpensive model that serves little purpose other than storing extra line. Most often, however, a short length of 10-pound-test monofilament is merely tied to the tip of the rod; the specific length of the line is of little consequence—personal preference rules—but for best control the rule of thumb is that it should never exceed the length of the pole.

To the terminal end of the line is tied a size 6 or 8 hook that is baited with a live minnow. Slightly above the hook a single split-shot is clamped onto the line. Still higher up, some variety of stand-up float is employed; those of European style described in Chapter 2 are effective.

In any event, with this outfit the experienced crappie angler is able to reach far out with his rod and meticulously work the outer edges of brush and tree limbs poking above the surface. Then, since no conventional casting is involved, he can with equal precision present his bait far back in tiny holes, channels, and other openings in the cover. Crappies inhale minnows very gingerly and therefore seldom pull a bobber all the way under; sometimes, even a featherweight float will barely twitch sideways.

The second, and equally deadly, spring crappie method involves the use of lightweight spinning tackle, a stand-up bobber, and a jig tied to the terminal end of the line. This is the outfit I select when crappies are spawning over woody bottom cover that does not protrude above the surface to such a degree that precise presentation of a bait is required. Now, 4-pound-test line is entirely adequate.

In murky water, I like jigs weighing from $\frac{1}{32}$ to $\frac{3}{32}$ ounce, with either marabou feathers or a tiny grub tail dressing the hook, and in bright two-tone colors such as yellow/chartreuse, yellow/white, blue/green, or pink/chartreuse. But in clear water I prefer all-white or all-yellow jigs with a live minnow tipping the hook.

The actual fishing technique is simple, fun, and yet so effective that even first-time anglers can master it in short order. Just make a long cast and allow the jig and bobber offering to sit motionless for several seconds. Then "pop" the bobber by making a short, quick flick of the wrist so the bobber darts forward several inches across the surface. This will cause the jig or jig and minnow combo to likewise "swim" forward several inches. A strike will usually come just at the very moment the offering ceases swimming and comes to a complete stop.

The all-important key to success with this method is the design of the stand-up bobber and interpreting its movements. After you've "popped" the bobber, carefully watch it for movement. Sometimes, a strike is registered by the bobber very slowly beginning to sink just a tad, usually no more than an inch or so. But even more frequently, a crappie rising from the bottom and inhaling the jig or the jig and minnow will take the weight of the lure off the bobber and thus cause it to momentarily lie down on its side. When this happens, set the hook gently and play your fish.

Incidentally, in shallow water, crappies spook quite easily at any unusual disturbance. This is why maintaining a cautious distance, through the use of long telescoping poles or by casting jigs and stand-up bobbers, is so effective.

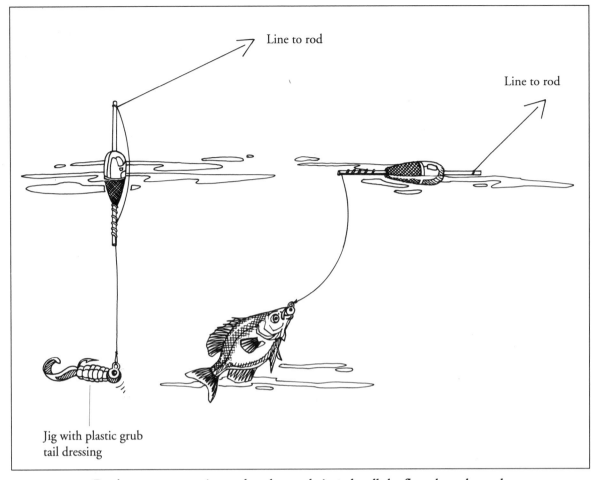

Line to rod

Line to rod

Jig with plastic grub
tail dressing

Don't expect a crappie to take a lure or bait and pull the float down beneath the surface. They more commonly rise with the offering, thus causing the float to lie down on the surface, signaling the strike.

STUMP-JUMPING IN SUMMER AND FALL

When white and black crappies conclude their spring spawning activities and begin returning to deeper water, look for them at depths generally ranging from twelve to twenty feet. For a while, these holding areas will undoubtedly be toward the mouths of the feeder tributaries and embayments where the fish previously spawned. But with each passing week the fish can be expected to move still closer and eventually into the main lake basin where still deeper water exists. And, since weeds generally do not grow at these depths, the fish predictably like to hang out near standing timber, deep stump fields, fallen logs and tree crowns on the bottom, and similar woody cover.

Now is when astute crappie anglers switch gears by putting away their telescoping panfish poles and using spinning or lightweight bait-casting tackle exclusively. And the technique which has been popularized in the last several decades is known as "stump-jumping." This entails briefly fishing jigs in the vicinity of such bottom cover described above and then, if no strikes are received, quickly moving on to the next likely looking place, and then the next.

A well-known strategy many crappie anglers

As summer approaches, crappies move into slightly deeper water yet continue to hang out near woody cover. Now the most effective technique, called "stump-jumping," is to cast lures close to the standing timber.

rely upon is constructing their own fishing hotspots. This is particularly effective on lakes where woody bottom cover is not extensive and the fish otherwise have a tendency to scatter and congregate in small groups where isolated cover does exist. In some instances the anglers gather discarded Christmas trees at the end of the holiday season, tie them together in bunches of three or four, tie to the assemblage a concrete block for weight, then drag the affair out onto the frozen lake in winter. When the ice melts in the spring, the crappie cover sinks. Minnows are attracted to the spot and feed upon the algae and moss that adhere to the branches, and crappies, after spawning, prey on the baitfish. If the lake in question doesn't freeze over in winter, anglers use boats to place the trees.

Weighted trees can even be placed from shore, along steep banks where the water depth abruptly drops off. In fact, many lakeshore homeowners have docks in their backyards and just off the ends of the docks sink Christmas trees, brush piles, or even stacked pallets or old tires tied together. The tip-off that such crappie cover exists will be bench seats or lawn chairs on the dock and one or two overhead lightposts, enabling the resident and his family to leisurely enjoy the evening hours fishing for crappies. Unless "No Fishing" signs are displayed on such docks, people don't seem to mind if a passing boat pauses to fish the cover because there are invariably enough crappies in the area to satisfy everyone who wants to try for them. As a result, many anglers make so-called "milk runs" in which the entire day is devoted exclusively to motoring

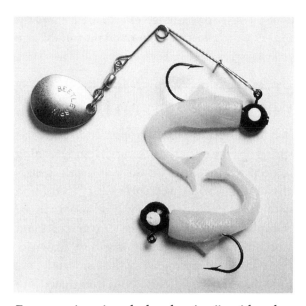

For stump-jumping, the best lure is a jig with a plastic twister tail that closely imitates a live minnow.

In lakes where suitable crappie cover is scant, anglers frequently make their own cover by submerging discarded Christmas trees along the shoreline. Crappies commonly move in to occupy the makeshift homes within hours.

their boats along the shoreline and stopping to fish at each dock which has overhead lights.

In stump-jumping, an angler's choice of jigs should be in the same color combinations recommended for spring-spawn fishing but considerably larger. Crappies are very size-conscious when it comes to taking one food item over another. Jigs weighing ⅛ to ¼ ounce and with slightly larger plastic, curly grub tails account for the largest. At this time of year, minnows have grown considerably and crappies seem to recognize the difference.

If the water depth does not exceed twelve feet or so, and is relatively clear, don't approach cover too closely as this may spook fish. This situation calls for casting, and I'm convinced the slowest possible retrieve is what crappies like best. Do not attempt to "reel" the lure in. Fish it just like a plastic worm for bass by casting, allowing the jig to sink, then retrieving it by very slowly raising the rod tip to the vertical position. When the rod tip is pointing straight up, quickly lower it, reel in the slack line this has generated, then repeat the slow upward raising of the rod tip. Be sure to work several different depths because if the stumps, logger-

Since crappies are attracted to woody cover in such great numbers, check dock pilings at marinas and the supporting framework of bridge and railway trestles.

heads, or other cover juts up from the bottom the fish may be holding at a specific level, and it's not characteristic of crappies to swim upward or downward more than two feet to capture their prey.

If the water depth exceeds twelve or fifteen

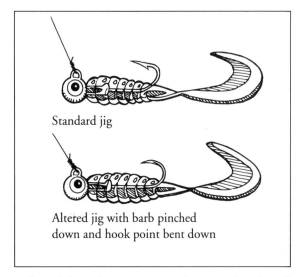

When fishing for crappies with jigs in brush and treetops, slightly bend the point of the hook downward and the lure will seldom snag.

When crappies are in deep stumps and treetops, anglers use depth sounders to locate the cover and then fish beneath the boat.

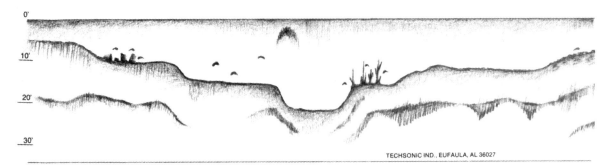

As midsummer approaches, crappies move into deeper water near stumps and standing trees along the edges of the old river channel winding along the bottom. This readout strip from a graph recorder shows crappies near such cover. The larger "hooks" suspended beneath the dark crescent are bass about to feed upon a surface-swimming school of baitfish.

feet, casting jigs becomes less and less effective because one loses control over the level at which the lure can be retrieved. Now is when expert crappie anglers like to position their boat directly over the cover and vertically jig for the fish. Simply lower the jig down into the cover, or around its edges, barely flick your wrist to make the jig dance around a bit, then hold it motionless in place. Again, test-fish a variety of depths to determine the particular level at which the crappies are holding on that particular day.

With either the casting or vertical-jigging technique, it might seem that your jig would repeatedly snag in the cover. There is a remedy for this.

Begin by pinching down the barb on the hook. Then, with pliers, bend the point of the hook down just a little so that its tip is pointing slightly toward the jig head. This little trick doesn't seem to hinder setting the hook, yet when the point is not quite so exposed it doesn't catch on twigs, branches, or bark so easily. Most of the time, because you're moving the jig very slowly anyway, it will come right through cover slick as a whistle. If the bend of the hook does perchance go around a tiny branch, or if the point digs into bark, simply jiggle your rod tip and it will usually fall free and you can continue working it.

Beginning sometime in midsummer, usually when the water temperature exceeds 65 degrees, crappies descend to very deep levels, often to depths of twenty-five to thirty-five feet. Their favorite hangouts are again woody cover, now found along the edges of sheer drop-offs or near old riverbed on the floor of the reservoir. Using a depth sounder and bottom-contour map is vital to finding the fish. Additionally, still another change in tackle and techniques is called for.

Since effectively using lightweight crappie jigs is difficult in such deep water, live minnow baits again reign supreme. Accomplished crappie anglers have developed a very novel way to fish them vertically directly beneath the boat.

The tackle called for now is a relatively long, 6- to 7-foot spinning rod with either an open- or closed-face reel, or a light-action baitcasting rod of the same length. Twenty-pound-test line is recommended, for reasons to be described shortly. Near the terminal end of the line two spreaders are attached, one above the other, so that two minnows can simultaneously be fished at slightly different depths. These spreaders are available in baitshops near popular crappie lakes, they can be purchased through mail-order shops, or you can make your own. To each spreader is tied a 6-inch length of 20-pound mono and then a thin-wire 3/0 Aberdeen hook. A ⅜-ounce egg-type sinker is then attached to the line about 12 inches above the top spreader.

Crappies, especially when they are in deep water, are not nearly as line-shy as many other panfish species and the heavy line in combination with the thin-wire hooks enables an angler to easily pull free from any treetops or brushy snags. This causes the lightweight hook to straighten out; later it can be reformed with pliers to its original shape.

The oversize sinker has several benefits. It adds tension to the rod to keep it in a slightly bowed or "loaded" position, which allows you to detect light bites; it keeps the heavy line straight and taut; and it enables you to fish in the windy and slightly choppy surface conditions which often are characteristic of midlake areas.

Using a brace of minnows increases your chances of quickly finding fish because you can fish two different depths simultaneously. Plus, with the minnows hooked lightly through the lips, which enables them to freely swim around, catching "doubles" is quite common. The two minnows swimming around seem to arouse a very competitive spirit in crappies, so once you detect a bite and set the hook, don't be too eager to reel in your fish. Keep the line tight and allow the crappie to swim around a bit and chances are good yet another crappie will grab the second minnow.

Since crappies gather in large schools during

If several crappies are caught in deep cover, throw overboard a floating marker to pinpoint the location of the fish. Then you can take your eyes off the depth sounder and concentrate on fishing.

with the intention of vertically fishing minnows in brush along the river channel edges but suddenly seeing the screen light up with untold numbers of suspended fish. Once such a joyous find is made, catching the crappies is relatively easy, but only if lures or bait are presented at the very level at which the crappies

midsummer, don't linger too long in a given location if you're not catching fish. Keep on the move, test-fishing a large number of the types of the locations described previously, and as soon as the first fish comes aboard you can be certain many more will follow. When you find a bonanza of fish near deep stumps or other cover in a wide-open, midlake region, it's wise to throw a marker buoy overboard so you don't have to continue watching the depth sounder and repositioning your boat over the hotspot.

In late summer and early fall, large schools of crappies also like to suspend at arbitrary mid-depths, generally in the vicinity of an old riverbed or over deep sand and gravel bars. Moreover, it's characteristic of them to hover on a horizontal plane within a very narrow depth range, almost like a waterlogged blanket floating in the water. In other words, the actual water depth may be fifty feet, with literally hundreds upon hundreds of crappies suspended between thirty-two to thirty-four feet.

Locating such schools of crappies is usually happenstance. It generally occurs when using a depth sounder and bottom contour map

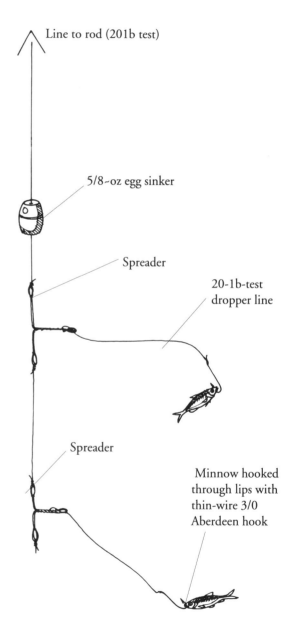

Line to rod (20lb test)

5/8-oz egg sinker

Spreader

20-lb-test dropper line

Spreader

Minnow hooked through lips with thin-wire 3/0 Aberdeen hook

When vertically fishing deep cover, most crappie anglers use a spreader rig and catch two fish at a time.

are suspended. First try lowering your minnow spreader rig to that depth level, just to make sure they really are crappies and not big gizzard shad or some such thing. Then, if fish begin coming aboard faster than you can re-bait your hooks, consider switching to artificials. Some anglers like to pump ⅜-ounce jigs or slab-sided jigging spoons. You can also troll small slim-minnow plugs such as the Rapala or Rebel, or straight-line spinners such as those made by Mepps, although you may have to experiment with weights attached to your line to reach the proper depth level.

NIGHT FISHING FOR CRAPPIES

Both white and black crappies feed voraciously after dark. And on popular crappie fishing lakes this means plenty of anglers become night owls by fishing directly from private docks, piers, bridges, or with boats positioned close to such structures. Strong lights play a key role in the success of nighttime crappie anglers.

When fishing from or near a private dock or any other structure which has no electric lights shining down toward the water, I like to use either a double-mantle gasoline or propane lantern because they emit brighter light than a battery-operated lantern. A shade or brim over the top of the globe, to reflect the greater portion of the light downward, makes these lanterns even more effective. From a camping supply store you can purchase metal clip-on lantern shades, or you can fashion a makeshift affair from heavy duty aluminum foil.

The bright light attracts plankton and other minute aquatic organisms as well as various forms of insects which in turn attract large schools of minnows. Shortly thereafter, schools of predator crappies can be expected to migrate in from nearby deep water to capitalize upon the abundance of food which has congregated within the glow of your light. Live minnows are

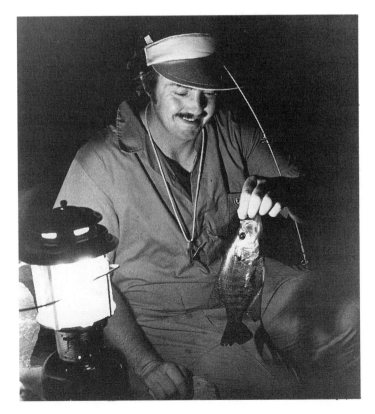

Crappies feed heavily after dark. A lantern not only provides illumination to see by, but also attracts schools of tiny minnows to the location, and crappies quickly move in to begin feeding.

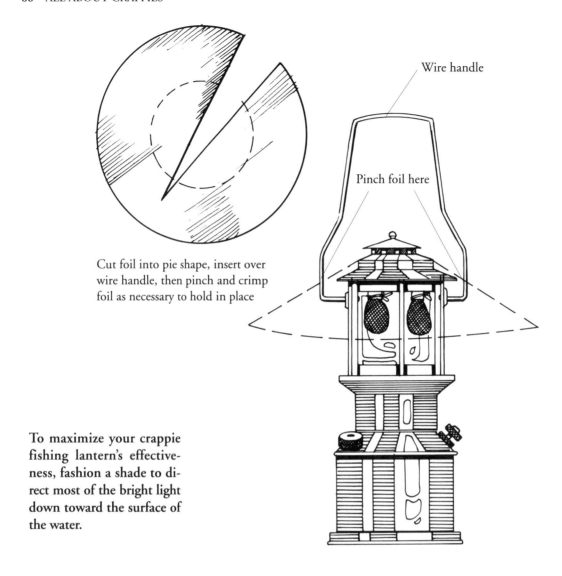

Cut foil into pie shape, insert over wire handle, then pinch and crimp foil as necessary to hold in place

Wire handle

Pinch foil here

To maximize your crappie fishing lantern's effectiveness, fashion a shade to direct most of the bright light down toward the surface of the water.

favored baits now, although jigs also produce, and the preferred methods of presentation are exactly the same as when the fish are spawning. Anglers hook a minnow just beneath a tiny bobber and fish it with a long telescoping panfish pole. Or they dangle a jig beneath a stand-up bobber cast with light spinning tackle and occasionally pop it to give it life.

7

White Bass Know-How

Did you ever dream about getting into such numbers of fish that you got a smashing strike on every cast?

Well, for tens of thousands of anglers every year this brand of fishing is not the product of imaginations gone wild. It's for real. The fish are feisty white bass, and I'm convinced this particular panfish affords the fastest freshwater fishing anyone could ever hope to experience.

When a concentration of white bass has been located, it is extremely common for everyone in the boat to be battling fish simultaneously. Mayhem typically follows, which is why it's always wise to have at least several rods rigged up and readily accessible. And don't bother to bring a stringer for there won't be time to secure individual fish on wire snaps. In this kind of panfishing, a fish brought aboard is quickly unhooked and then tossed in the direction of an open cooler with one hand while the other is zinging out another cast. If your line breaks or tangles, or something else goes wrong with your tackle, lay it aside and grab another pre-rigged rod; you can make repairs or new riggings later. I call it blitz bass fishing because everything

White bass afford the fastest and most exciting freshwater fishing. It's common to receive a jarring strike on every cast!

The white bass is closely related to the much larger striped bass. The species is common in large reservoirs where the water depth does not exceed thirty feet.

happens so fast. Yet, since each action period is not likely to last too long, it's imperative to maximize each opportunity to put fish in the boat. It reminds me of those television quiz shows in which a contestant has a limited amount of time to stuff his pockets with cash.

Sometimes known regionally as *stripes, sandies,* or *silver bass,* white bass are members of the *Morone chrysops* family, which means they are true bass and very closely related to striped bass, yellow bass, and white perch.

The most distinguishing features of the species are its silver-white sides highlighted by dark, lateral stripes extending from the gill covers to the tail. The ventral region usually is pure white, and the dorsal region is bluish-olive in color.

The original range of the white bass was limited to the upper Midwest and, in particular, the Great Lakes and the Mississippi and St. Lawrence River systems. However, when the Army Corp of Engineers and the Tennessee Valley Authority began damming major river systems and constructing mammoth impoundments to generate hydroelectric power in the early 1940s, white bass were routinely planted in the giant reservoirs to control baitfish populations. Since then, their presence has mush-

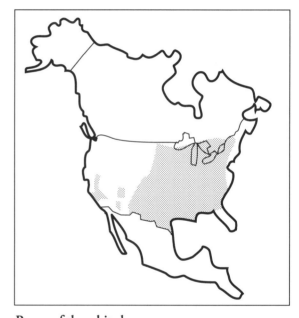

Range of the white bass.

roomed and nowadays, with the exception of New England, all states east of the Continental Divide have impressive white bass populations, as do several western states such as California, Arizona, Nevada, and Utah.

The world-record white bass, taken in 1977 in Texas, weighed 5- pounds, and every year 3- and 4-pounders are relatively common. The

During the spring spawning period, enormous schools of white bass frequently congregate in tailrace waters just below dams.

In main-lake areas, white bass move into feeder tributaries in the spring. Fish only those tributaries that have a distinct current flowing through them.

great majority of fish, however, average 12 to 16 inches in length and weigh approximately 1 to 2 pounds.

Like many other panfish species, white bass are extremely prolific. Yet certain bodies of water offer far superior white bassing than others.

The greatest likelihood of finding a white bass bonanza will be on an impoundment ranging from 20,000 to 100,000 acres in size. It will also be a body of water fed by at least one major river system and several smaller feeder tributaries. Further, the average water depth will not exceed thirty feet, and the bottom composition will be firm, made up of hard-packed clay, sand, shell, limestone, granite, or any combination of these materials. But, unquestionably, since the diet of white bass consists almost exclusively of small fish, the body of water's most notable attribute will be a very large and self-sustaining baitfish population. This forage may consist of virtually any minnow, chub, or dace species, but white bass are especially partial to gizzard and threadfin shad that average 1- to 3 inches in length.

EARLY SPRING FISHING

White bass fishing action begins in very early spring when the water temperature approaches 55 degrees and the fish leave their deep-water winter homes in the main-lake basin areas and begin swarming into feeder rivers, streams, and creek arms for the purposes of spawning. In the largest manmade reservoirs, enormous populations of white bass also frequently gather in the tailrace just below the downstream dam responsible for impounding the water.

White bass do not construct spawning nests. Rather, females release their eggs into the water while males simultaneously release milt. The fertilized eggs then settle to the bottom where they stick to rocks or sparse vegetation for an incubation period of forty-eight hours before the young fry hatch.

I have seen white bass so thick in these tributaries that their overcrowding actually had the effect of now and then forcing individual fish out of the water and up onto the banks, whereupon they momentarily flip-flopped around until eventually landing back in the water. The types

**Finding large numbers of spawning white bass in feeder tributaries is easy.
Just look for other anglers!**

In the shallowest tributaries, where boat control would be difficult, wade-fishing is the recommended technique. White bass are aggressive feeders, so use artificial lures rather than live bait.

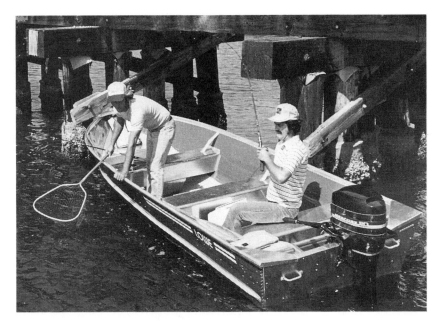

When spawning is completed, white bass move out of the tributaries and back into main-lake areas. For several weeks they'll hang around shoreline gravel bars, points, and manmade structures such as docks and bridge pilings.

of feeder tributaries I look for are ones that have a distinct current running through them and have an average depth of three to six feet. If in doubt, a sure tip-off that white bass action is heating up in a given tributary will be the presence of numerous other anglers lining the banks.

Since it can be difficult to control a small boat in the constantly flowing current while simultaneously handling a rod that begins to buck and throb every few minutes, I like to wade-fish or hike along the banks to cast into eddy-water, pools, and glides.

I suggest light tackle because white bass are real scrappers. Their battles are even more exciting if you don't overpower them with heavy gear. The outfit I use is a medium-light spinning rod 6 feet in length. Mounted on the rod is an open-face reel loaded to capacity with 6-pound monofilament line.

Since white bass are prone to so savagely mauling artificial lures, most anglers simply don't care to be bothered with rigging live baits to catch the species.

When selecting artificial lures for white bass, keep in mind that they feed voraciously upon minnow life, so your lures should mimic small baitfish. Wise choices include spinners, spoons, and small plugs measuring no more than 2 inches in length, weighing ¼ to ⅜ ounce, and in mullet blue, shad gray, and silver colors. Also extremely effective are ¼-ounce, all-white jigs sporting plastic twister tails in lieu of bucktail or feather dressings.

As the spawning season draws to a close, white bass begin drifting out of the feeder streams and tributaries and back into the main-lake areas and for brief weeks can easily be located in shallow water. You'll find them grouping rather loosely at the mouths of the creeks, along adjacent shorelines, on points of land that extend out into the lake and continue underwater, and around bridge pilings where roads parallel the shoreline. Be especially on the lookout for shallow sandbars and gravel shoals near these shoreline areas because such places attract baitfish and consequently the white bass as well.

Since the fish are now fairly well dispersed, you'll chance upon several here, a few somewhere else, and so on. For this kind of fishing I prefer to drift-fish while randomly casting around likely looking areas. When I catch one fish, I quietly let down the anchor or hold the boat in position with an electric motor and continue working the immediate area, often catching several more before deciding to try elsewhere.

At this time of year, I recommend working your lures two to six feet deep as this is the level at which most of the fish will be cruising in search of food. And, as is the case with any type of early-season fishing, work your lures relatively slowly because the water in these main-lake areas is still cool and the fish are not nearly as active as they will be in weeks to come.

There is one other type of shallow shoreline water that is extremely productive during the late spring/early summer period, and that is wherever you can find wind and wave action buffeting the bank and creating choppy surface conditions. The white bass's favorite food—shad and other baitfish—are customarily surface-swimming species, and the turbulent water pushes them against the banks. In effect, they become trapped against a wall, which leaves them vulnerable to various predators. The white bass seem to know this instinctively and move in for an easy meal.

This type of fishing ideally calls for the use of a bow-mounted electric motor, operated by a remote foot-control pedal, so you can stand in the front of the craft and have both hands free to make long casts as you methodically work parallel to the windswept shoreline.

SUMMER AND FALL FISHING

As the season progresses into July, the fish move far away from their former shallow haunts, gather

During midsummer and fall, white bass become nomads and wander endlessly. They especially like to travel the length of the old riverbed on the floor of a reservoir. Best way to find a school of white bass is to locate a school of baitfish. The whites are sure to be close to their favorite forage.

in enormous schools that sometimes number in the thousands, and roam vast mid-lake areas until as late as October, or even November in the deep South. Now, finding the fish becomes more difficult because they may travel several miles in a single twenty-four-hour period. They do not travel in haphazard fashion, however, but engage in trailing-migration patterns designed to keep tabs upon large baitfish schools that are similarly on the move. Consequently, if you can find baitfish schools, a school of white bass will undoubtedly be nearby.

Homing-in upon baitfish is relatively easy because they are quite predictable. During the course of their never-ending search for their favorite food—plankton—they like to follow "routes," or structures. A prime example of such a travel corridor is an inundated riverbed on the floor of an impoundment. Use your map to investigate old roadbeds and railroad spurs that have become covered with water when the impoundment filled; these appear like tentacles of underwater ridges that, due to their rock foundations, elevate them from adjacent areas.

Interestingly, the movements of white bass following baitfish are much the same as a beagle hot on the trail of a cottontail. For example, the bait-

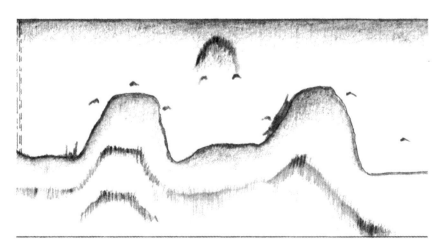

This actual readout strip from a graph recorder shows white bass traveling the length of an old riverbed. Some of the fish are actually feeding in a school of baitfish, indicated by the dark crescent near the surface.

Once you find a school of baitfish or white bass, throw out a marker buoy to pinpoint their location.

Understandably, a bit of guesswork and random searching is usually necessary at the outset because one never knows exactly where the fish are located along the length of their route. In fact, a travel corridor that extends for many miles downlake may well see the presence of several dozen individual schools of white bass following their respective prey.

So I recommend motoring open, mid-lake areas, methodically checking those long and clearly defined structures that the fish are likely to be traveling along. Moreover, it's virtually impossible to do this without a bottom contour map and some type of depth sounder.

Once the particular bottom structure has been located and I've oriented myself to it, I keep my eyes continually glued to the sonar screen before me and watch for the boat to pass over a school of baitfish. On a flashing-type depth sounder they usually appear on the whirring neon dial as a solid band of red light at a depth of from zero to about five feet beneath the surface. On a liquid crystal display unit or graph recorder they will appear as a solid band of gray. In fact, many times you'll simultaneously see the white bass themselves directly beneath the baitfish. On a flashing-type depth sounder they will appear as numerous, individual

fish may travel the entire length of the lake, following the old riverbed. Eventually they reach the dam, turn, and then travel back in the opposite direction to the other end of the lake, only to reverse themselves and travel the route again.

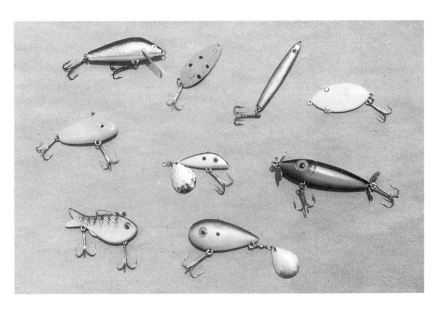

Popular lures for white bass include spoons, spinners, and plugs that represents minnows.

WHITE BASS KNOW-HOW 95

"spikes" of red light. On an LCD or graph recorder they'll appear as numerous "hooks" or crescents at a depth of anywhere from ten to twenty feet beneath the baitfish.

There are two ways to catch white bass once you've located them. The first, if they are deep, is to vertically pump jigs, leadhead tailspinner lures, or slablike jigging spoons. Lower the lures directly beneath the boat to the same depth as the fish, slowly raise them four or five feet, and then let them flutter back down by slowly lowering your rod tip. Most of the time, strikes will come as the lure is sinking.

JUMP-FISHING

A good time to catch white bass is when a school rises to the surface and slashes into a school of baitfish. Sometimes an entire square acre of water will erupt in frothy foam as the whites attempt to force the bait against the surface. The fish work themselves into such a feeding frenzy that it's extremely common for them to gorge their bellies and then regurgitate their contents so they can continue feeding.

The standard fishing technique, called *jump-fishing,* is to ease your boat cautiously close to the surface-feeding action and make long casts. Use the same shad-imitating lures recommended earlier and retrieve them with short jerks and twitches to simulate a struggling, injured baitfish.

Each of these surface-feeding periods will be relatively short-lived (generally, no longer than five minutes) before the white bass, fully sated, return to their former suspended depth, so get into the action as quickly as possible.

During this entire episode, the baitfish and white bass usually remain on the move. So in most cases it is necessary to keep your electric

Anglers glass distant areas in hopes of finding flocks of birds gathering over the water. When they spot birds, it means surface-feeding action is about to begin.

motor turned on "high" speed to keep up with them as they continue to travel downlake along the length of their migration route.

When the surface feeding eventually comes to a conclusion, study your map to reorient yourself with the old river channel, roadbed, or other structure the fish are migrating along. Then race ahead in a wide arc to try to intercept the fish at some point farther along their presumed direction of travel. You may have to motor as far as a half-mile before the baitfish and suspended white bass reappear on your depth sounder. At that time, you can begin jigging for the deep fish while waiting for them to come to the surface.

WATCH THE BIRDS

Jump-fishing requires a boat equipped with an outboard of at least modest horsepower. In fact,

on the largest impoundments, white bass anglers commonly make use of 16- to 18-foot craft of the so-called "bassboat" genre equipped with outboards of 100 horsepower or more. They also rely upon birds to tell them where distant surface-feeding activity is taking place.

The birds generally are high-soaring gulls, terns, or kingfishers which keep tabs on surface-swimming schools of baitfish. When white bass periodically rise from the depths to slash into the prey, the scavenging birds then begin swooping and diving to the surface to pick up broken bits and pieces of the mauled shad.

Strong binoculars are required to glass distant areas for signs of birds beginning to gather. Then the race is on to close the distance and make a dozen or so casts before the feeding episode is over. Still again, do not race headlong right into the surface-feeding activi-

When the white bass begin feeding, the birds dive to the surface to pick up mauled baitfish. Anglers then race to the scene and catch fish on every cast.

Once the white bass have concluded their surface feeding and once again retreated into the depths, many additional fish can be caught by vertically fishing jigs and jigging spoons.

ty. Remain around the perimeter and make long casts to avoid spooking the fish.

While you're watching for birds, keep an eye on distant boats as well. If several of them suddenly begin racing in a given direction, feel free to join the show because they've probably spotted birds diving to the surface that you couldn't see from your location. On the largest reservoirs where jump-fishing is popular, it's

quite common for strangers on the water to cooperate in this manner.

In coming weeks, however, most white bass action will cease. As the water temperature drops into the 55-degree range, the predators will descend into deep water, usually the depths of the old riverbed, and with ever-slowing body metabolisms will await the rituals of spring courtship.

8

Rock Bass Basics

The nemesis of dedicated smallmouth bass and walleye anglers is the rock bass. All three species occupy the same habitat. Since the rock bass is an extremely aggressive panfish, it typically beats larger gamefish in the race to grab a lure or bait.

In fact, there have been more times than I can remember when smallmouths and walleyes were the target species of the day but rock bass frustrated anglers in my boat by constantly taking their offerings.

Yet here is the intriguing paradox of all of this. On many occasions, were it not for rock bass, we wouldn't have caught a thing at all. And I can remember as many outings in which everyone in camp was looking forward to an eventful fish fry at day's end, and it was the otherwise disparaged rock bass that saved the day.

In addition, when taken on lightweight tackle the rock bass puts up such a good fight that it has become one of my favorite panfish.

As is the case with the smallmouth and largemouth bass, the rock bass is not a true bass but a member of the sunfish family. And his Latin

Many anglers after larger fish such as walleyes often hook rock bass. Sometimes confused with the warmouth, it is a worthy fish in its own right.

Range of the rock bass.

name, *Ambloplites rupestris,* which means "living among the rocks," describes exactly where to find the species.

Rock bass have several distinguishing physical features, the most prominent of which is a larger mouth than any other sunfish. Nature gave rock bass oversize maws because the females produce only a small number of eggs compared to other panfish. When diligently defending their spawning beds, male rock bass continually open and close their mouths and flare their gill covers, giving the illusion of having a much larger head. It has been suggested that this may intimidate other fish that might be inclined to rush into the nesting area to devour the offspring, and thus ensures the survival of a large number of them.

The rock bass also has a large, crimson-colored eye, which explains its popular nicknames *goggleye* and *redeye.*

Even though these specific body features should allow unfailing identification of the species, the rock bass is sometimes mistaken for other panfish because of its chameleon-like ability to change its body coloration to match the color of its rocky habitat. The usual color of the fish is greenish-olive with each scale revealing a rectangular-shaped, brown spot that gives it a mottled appearance. Yet within just a few minutes the rock bass can change to light green, bronze, or almost solid black, the latter phase being responsible for still another nickname, *black perch.* The method of positive identification used by biologists is to count the number of spines in the dorsal fin; the rock bass has eleven.

The original range of the rock bass was the eastern United States and eastern Canadian provinces. But transplanting programs have spread the fish's range throughout the Midwest, into Oklahoma, Texas, New Mexico, and Arizona, and even into portions of Washington and Oregon.

Rock bass thrive in cool, clean waters. As the name of the species implies, rock bass and rocks go together like bacon and eggs.

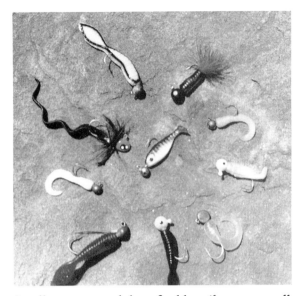

In all seasons, rock bass feed heavily upon small minnows, crayfish, and leeches. Lures should therefore mimic those favorite foods.

The species thrives in lakes, reservoirs, and rivers. Although the world record for rock bass is shared by a brace of 3-pounders, one from Ontario and the other from Indiana, and although rock bass are far more plentiful in northern waters, southern streams and rivers produce larger fish on the average. In fact, in the deep South, 2-pounders are relatively common, undoubtedly because of the warmer water and longer annual growing season; elsewhere, adult rock bass average 8 inches in length and ¾ pound in weight.

Yet no matter where they are found, rock bass thrive in clean, clear water where the bottom is made up of rocks, boulders, gravel, sand, or any combination of these hard materials. The species is tolerant of sparse weed growth, and upon occasion even uses thin vegetation during

Throughout the South, rock bass are more commonly found in rivers than in lakes.

LOCATING ROCK BASS

Submerged bar is too rounded and smooth to attract many rock bass

Rock piles attract more fish

Angular rocks and slabs with pronounced features are best of all because of more hiding places for baitfish and crayfish

the spring spawning season. Rock bass do not do well in waters where thick, matted weed growth appears as the season progresses.

SPRING SPAWNING

In the northern areas of their range, rock bass generally engage in mating activities during the months of May and June or whenever the water temperature climbs above the 65-degree mark. Yet biologists have always been puzzled that rock bass in the southern areas of their range seem to require cooler water. In streams and rivers, mating usually occurs when the water is only 55 to 60 degrees.

Unlike bluegills and other sunfish, rock bass do not nest in large colonies. You cannot stand in the bow of your boat and spot their beds in shallow water. Instead, rock bass tend to drift into the shallows in loose groups, fan out rudimentary saucer-shaped depressions in water less than four feet deep, and then quickly get on with the business of reproducing their kind. One tip for locating spawning rock bass is that their nests are typically swept out on a sand or gravel bottom in wind-protected coves or along lee shorelines. Moreover, they like to situate their nests up against something like a log, stump, boulder, or newly emerging vegetation such as a reed bank or stand of bulrushes.

Since rock bass are very defensive of their spawning sites, there really is no need to bother with live bait. The fish will savagely attack artificial lures time and again, even if your boat is inadvertently allowed to drift to within scant feet of their shallow-water spawning areas.

As a result, lures that resemble small, intruding fish are first-rate choices. Many anglers enjoy using medium-action flyrods, reels filled with sinking-tip lines, and brightly colored streamer flies such as the Mickey Finn or White Marabou.

Or, if you prefer, arm yourself with light spinning tackle, 4 pound-test line and ¼ ounce singlespin spinnerbaits in white or yellow. Other lethal lures include straight-shaft spinners and ⅜ ounce jigs. Use all-white jigs dressed with white curlytail grubs and retrieve them in a slow swimming manner to represent minnows. Or, use orange or brown jigs with bucktail dressing to simulate crayfish and slowly bump them across the bottom in the vicinity of bedding areas.

SUMMER AND FALL

Since the habitat preferences of rock bass during summer and fall are identical to those of the walleye and smallmouth, locating the fish is likewise virtually the same. In fact, since panfish in a given body of water always outnumber gamefish species, finding rock bass is unquestionably easier. What I mean is, if you know the locations of ten rocky bars or reefs, for example, and they all look like suitable walleye habitat, chances are that you would actually find walleyes on perhaps only two of them but that you'd find rock bass on all ten!

They especially seem to like those types of bottom contours that are situated in deep water but jut up to within several feet of the surface. They also have an undeniable preference for slab rocks that have well-defined features such as sharp angular sides and ends, compared to other rocky bottom features which are more rounded and smooth on top. My guess is that the reason for this preference is because rock bass generally feed on or near the bottom and jumbled rock formations offer greater hiding opportunities for crayfish, snails, hellgrammites, minnows, and other bottom-dwelling lifeforms.

Rock bass also like to hang along underwater ledge formations and shoreline drop-offs and shelves that, at their outermost edges, rapidly give way to deep water.

In all of these instances, a bottom contour map and depth sounder can be invaluable tools for finding suitable rock bass habitat. But if you have neither, your eyes alone can usually steer you in the right direction.

First, begin looking for rubble-strewn shorelines, but not the continuous variety that travel

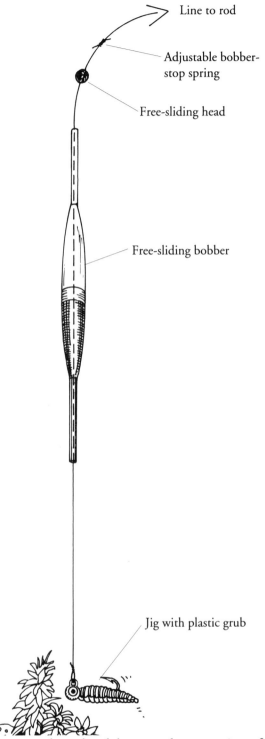

Line to rod

Adjustable bobber-stop spring

Free-sliding head

Free-sliding bobber

Jig with plastic grub

Bottom rocks and rock bass may be at a variety of depths. The most effective way to catch the species is with a jig fished beneath a slip-bobber rig that can be adjusted to the proper depth.

Rock bass do not travel much. Suitable locations that produce fish one day will produce still more for many days and weeks to come.

endlessly for miles. Rather, search for brief stretches no more than 100 yards in length because the isolated nature of the structure will tend to concentrate the fish.

Tapered shoreline points are another good bet, especially those littered with rocks and which extend far out from the shoreline before dropping off abruptly at their tip ends into deep water.

Generally, during the summer and fall, the fish consort in loose groups at depths ranging from six to twenty-five feet. Since rock bass are quite light sensitive, they engage in the bulk of their feeding activities early and late in the day and after full dark. During midday when bright sunlight is penetrating the water, the fish descend into deeper water and are far less active.

Since the feeding behavior of rock bass is so aggressive, I suggest using artificial lures rather than live bait.

If you elect to use live bait, the best all-around offering is a leech, hooked once through the sucker, or a worm or small minnow hooked once through the head. Then,

backtroll the offering with a Lindy-rig of the very same type used for perch and described in Chapter 9.

Another top notch bait is crayfish tail meat. Simply break the tail from the body, peel the shell away, split the tail meat lengthwise into two pieces, and then impale one at a time on a jig hook or the hook of a straight-shaft spinner.

In the artificial lure category, it's difficult to beat a jig and slip-bobber rig. This is essentially nothing more than a jig dressed with a swimming grub tail. The stand-up variety with an anvil-shaped head is preferred over a round-head because it does not snag as frequently in the crevices of rocky bottom structures. Tie the jig to the end of your line; above, thread on a free-sliding bobber; then, just above the bobber, thread on a tiny plastic bead, and finally an adjustable "bobber stop" spring which securely grips the line. Slip-bobbers are discussed in greater detail in Chapter 2.

As an alternative to a slip-bobber rig, you can of course simply cast the jig in the conventional manner and slowly bounce it across the bottom.

Other lures which are popular among rock bass anglers on lakes and reservoirs are $\frac{1}{4}$- to $\frac{3}{8}$-ounce crankbaits. These are merely plugs that resemble small minnows and panfish and have wide, slanted bills protruding from their noses which cause them to dive deeply on the retrieve. They can be highly effective whenever rock bass are less than twelve feet deep.

In rivers and streams, anglers customarily use very light spinning tackle to cast straight-shaft spinners or jigs adorned with plastic curlytails in gravel riffles and along rock-strewn shorelines. Fly-rodders also enjoy superb action using the bright-colored streamer flies described earlier for the shallows.

Finally, it's worth mentioning that rock bass do not travel around much in the given body of water they inhabit. After spawning, they typically abandon the shallows for the nearest suitable summer/fall habitat that satisfies their food needs and water depth preferences and seem content to live and loaf right there for the remainder of the open-water months.

As a result, anglers frequently establish what are known as "milk runs" consisting of a number of known locations where there are rock bass and then each day repeatedly visiting one after another. Eventually, however, the water will gradually begin cooling in late fall, and when it reaches 50 degrees rock bass descend into deep holes and slip into a dormant stage until the following spring.

9

Yellow Perch

Some types of fishing are downright complicated, taxing your skills to the limit. Then there are yellow perch, which are a splendid example of fun fish I like to catch. Here's the way the scenario generally plays itself out.

On a balmy spring afternoon I'll take a john-boat or aluminum v-bottom onto a lake. My tackle consists of nothing more elaborate than a lightweight spinning rod or two, a little plastic box of size 8 hooks, several plastic bobbers, and a pail of minnows. Likely as not, I'll have a small cooler onboard, amply stocked with sandwiches and cold drinks, and perhaps there will even be a small portable radio sitting on one of the seats, tuned to some ballgame or other.

Then I'll motor to the protected lee side of the lake and begin searching for just one telltale clue that perch are around; I'll relate that clue in

Many claim the yellow perch is our most delicious panfish. Best of all, the species is relatively easy to catch in large numbers.

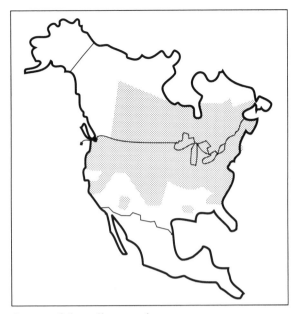

Range of the yellow perch.

a moment. Invariably, by day's end, I'll be sun-burned on the back of the neck and yet fully contented as I return to the dock with more than enough fish to keep my family well fed for weeks to come. To me, this is panfishing at its finest, and so it's not surprising that, nation-wide, yellow perch attract legions of other an-glers as well.

Yellow perch average less than 10 inches in length and have an elongated rather than a dish-shaped body profile like bluegills or crappies. However, it's common for the species to reach 12 to 15 inches in length, in which case anglers frequently refer to them as *jumbo perch* or *jack perch*. The world record perch weighed slightly over 4 pounds and was caught way back in 1865 in a small lake in New Jersey.

In some regions, the species is also known as *ringed perch* or raccoon perch because its basic body coloration of golden olive is accen-tuated by six to nine greenish-black vertical stripes. Other distinguishing features include a forked tail and a humped forehead just be-hind the eyes.

It's important to note that perch are school

fish. Studies by Wisconsin biologists have re-vealed that most schools contain between 50 and 300 fish. Moreover—and here is one of the most important tips to keep in mind—perch are very size-oriented in their schooling tenden-cies. Therefore, if you're catching only small fish, do not hesitate to try elsewhere in search of a school that may very well be comprised of much larger individuals.

The perch's original range was limited to the Canadian border states and, with the exception of British Columbia, all of the provinces. But the species has long since been transplanted far beyond its native habitat and now can be found even as far south as Georgia, across the heart-land of the United States and down into New Mexico and California. Yellow perch are also found in all of the Great Lakes, except Lake Su-perior, in most of the large river drainages of the upper midwestern states, and in most of the tidal rivers that drain into the Atlantic from Nova Scotia to South Carolina.

Yellow perch do best in moderately cool, clean waters where the lake basin is largely comprised of rock and sand. If a given lake has pike, muskies, walleyes, or smallmouth bass, perch are likely to be the predominating panfish species.

As with most fish species, young perch forage upon zooplankton, small insects, and aquatic larvae. Yet detailed studies of the stomach con-tents of adult perch over 6 inches in length have revealed their distinct preference for minnows (primarily darters, shiners and sticklebacks) not exceeding 2 inches in length.

As to their most active feeding periods, and therefore the best times of day for anglers to be on the water, yellow perch engage in relatively mild-mannered feeding activities during the first two hours after sun-up. Then there is a characteristic lull in their feeding until some-time in midafternoon when the action once again begins to pick up. There seems to be a consensus among most experienced perch fishermen that the prime time of day to catch their quarry is from about 3 p.m. until dusk. Then, since yellow perch, unlike their walleye cousins, cannot see well after dark, feeding activity abruptly ceases shortly after the sun sets.

Another aspect of perch behavior is their water-depth preferences. In early spring they may be as shallow as three feet, in late summer as deep as 30 feet. However, the rule of thumb is that whenever perch are deeper than 12 feet, for whatever the reason, they will virtually always be holding within a foot of the bottom. Conversely, whenever the water is shallower than 12 feet, they may be arbitrarily swimming around at any depth level, particularly if weed growth is present, although they rarely spend much time within two feet of the surface.

SPRING FISHING

A sure-fire way to find large numbers of yellow perch in the spring is to locate their spawning grounds. Spawning occurs when the water temperature is within the range of 44 to 54 degrees F, and the mating activity generally takes place in protected coves, embayments, feeder tribu-

taries, and on the lee sides of shoreline points and shallow reefs. Virtually all spawning is done during the night, when each female, flanked by numerous males, releases consecutive strings of eggs into the milt-clouded water. The fertilized eggs form translucent, jelly-like masses called egg strands, each of which averages an inch wide by 6 inches in length and may contain upward of 25,000 eggs.

Gentle breezes have a tendency to push these egg masses shoreward, where, due to their sticky nature, they cling to brush, sticks, rocks, weedstems, and other shallow-water cover for a prescribed incubation period before hatching into fry. These egg strands are readily visible to even the casual observer hiking along the bank or slowly motoring along the shoreline and, once located, indicate the presence of adult fish nearby.

Since spawning occurs at night, midday sees the perch holding in water that is generally no more than five to ten feet deep and seldom more than fifty yards offshore. There, they bide their time, feeding sometimes ravenously as they await darkness and yet another inshore spawning flurry.

Incidentally, these same spawning grounds are visited by perch year after year. So, although

To find yellow perch in spring, motor slowly along shallow shorelines and look for their jelly-like egg strands clinging to brush, rocks, and weedstems.

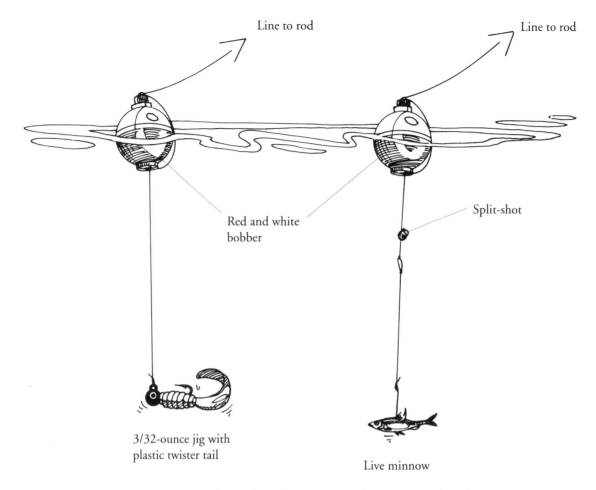

Line to rod

Line to rod

Red and white bobber

Split-shot

3/32-ounce jig with plastic twister tail

Live minnow

Once egg strands are located, randomly cast a bobber rigged with a jig dressed with a plastic twister tail or a hook baited with a live minnow.

your initial effort in locating several such places may require a good deal of exploratory work, every year thereafter you know exactly where to find fish.

The perfect tackle combination for this kind of fishing consists of nothing more than a lightweight spinning outfit and either an open- or closed-face reel filled with 4- or 6-pound-test monofilament. To the terminal end of the line, tie a size-8 long-shanked hook, clamp a tiny split-shot onto the line, and bait up with a 2-inch minnow. A small red and white plastic bobber of no more than 1 inch in diameter should be positioned on your line at the mid-level of the water depth at that location; in other words, if the water is approximately six feet deep, affix your bobber so that your bait is presented three feet beneath the surface.

Although you can anchor and lob-cast your offering randomly around your boat, with an electric trolling motor you can slowly maneuver around or momentarily hold the craft in position so the wind does not push you too quickly shoreward.

I mentioned earlier that I usually have at least two rods onboard. The second outfit is rigged in an identical manner with the exception that,

When spawning is completed, perch usually remain near shoreline structures for several months. Shoreline points and rubble-littered banks are favorite hangouts.

instead of a hook I tie on a $\frac{3}{32}$-ounce jig sporting an inch-long plastic split-tail trailer. Colors such as yellow, white, and orange, or any combination of these hues, seem to work best.

It's wise to begin fishing with live bait since the spawning fish, when they are holding slightly offshore during midday, are usually loosely scattered. Yet quite often you'll find them bunched up in large numbers and continually rebaiting your hook can become tiresome, whereas switching to an artificial allows you to capitalize upon the momentary fast action by landing as many fish as possible with the least amount of effort. If there is the slightest amount of wind and wave action, this will give the jig's plastic tail a swimming action. But if the water is calm, maintain a tight line and occasionally wiggle the rod tip.

Whether using live minnows for bait, or jigs, don't expect a yellow perch to aggressively smack your offering and pull your bobber entirely beneath the surface. More often you'll barely see the bobber twitch and that is the time to strike.

SUMMER AND FALL PERCH FISHING

When spawning activity is completed, yellow perch generally linger in the immediate vicinity for several weeks and anglers can continue catching them using the same methods described earlier. Yet when the fish ultimately abandon their spawning grounds, where they spend the remainder of the year is invariably determined by the personality of the lake they inhabit and, thus, the available cover and span of water temperatures over the months.

In the deeper, colder lakes of the northern border states, yellow perch may remain shoreline-oriented in the months to come because there simply is no need for them to venture into deep, offshore haunts to find their preferred 65-degree temperature range. This often means gathering in large numbers along the edges of weedbeds where the water depth abruptly drops off.

In such waters, perch also like to congregate in large numbers in the deeper portions of shallow embayments where there are thick fields of coontail, cabomba and cabbage weeds at depths of six to ten feet. Also check tapering shoreline points littered with gravel and chunk rock which extend out from the bank and then continue long distances underwater before dropping off steeply at their tip ends.

In somewhat shallower, and therefore warmer, lakes yellow perch may move considerable distances from their spawning grounds. As we discuss this particular type of habitat, however, keep in mind that a lake described as shallow or warm doesn't automatically imply a body of water along the southernmost reaches of the yellow perch's range. Lake Erie, for example, is a relatively warm lake much of the year where the average depth is only 14 feet and yet it is one of the most popular perch-fishing lakes in the country.

In these larger bodies of water, which in places may be several miles wide, it may initially seem like a foreboding task to find concentrations of yellow perch. But actually, that isn't the case at all, because of the predictable nature of the species.

Consequently, insightful anglers need only briefly study a bottom contour map and the summer/fall haunts of perch should be readily evident.

Look for offshore structures that rise from the bottom to within several feet of the surface and which are comprised of slab rock, boulders, gravel, sand or any combination of these hard materials. Anglers commonly refer to these types of bottom structures by a variety of names, including reefs, shoals, bars or sunken islands.

Although these structures are essentially pretty much the same, and all may be attractive to yellow perch, some are distinctly more productive than others. I particularly like the largest structures, which commonly may be a hundred square yards or larger in size. And I especially like those which have one or more steeply sloping sides or other sharply defined features. This diversity in bottom configuration offers perch a variety of depth levels and foraging opportunities and thereby is attractive to greater numbers of fish than a similar-sized structure which may be only gently undulating in appearance.

PRESENTATION IS THE KEY

An especially lethal method for catching perch is the Lindy-rigging method developed by Al and Ron Lindner of Brainerd, Minnesota. A Lindy-rig is assembled by first threading a sliding sinker onto the line. Generally, a ¼-ounce sinker is best for starters; then, if necessary, switch to a lighter or heavier sinker in accordance with the water depth. Now, tie the terminal end of the line to a small barrel swivel. After that, tie a second length of line, four feet in length, to the opposite end of the barrel swivel. To the terminal end of this "leader" tie a size 10 hook.

Ideal baits for perch when Lindy-rigging include small nightcrawlers, leeches and small minnows hooked just once through the head,

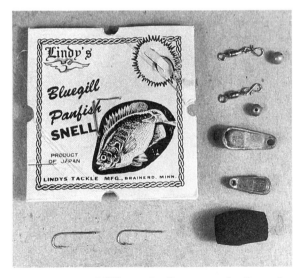

In summer and fall, perch often move far from the banks near weeds, reefs, shoals, and sunken rock-capped islands. Trolling with a Lindy-rig is the most effective means of catching them. Shown here are the basic components.

or tiny crayfish hooked just once through the tail. Now, since no casting is involved, pay out line until the rig hits bottom directly beneath and slightly behind your boat and begin very slowly trolling and bouncing the bait along the bottom. Use an electric motor for the slowest possible speed, or run your outboard in reverse so the broad transom of the boat, rather than the bow, is pushing into the water in the direction you wish to fish, to retard the boat's speed.

A medium-action spinning rod with an open-face spinning reel is best for this kind of work and 4-pound-test line is recommended. Keep the reel's bail open, with your finger curled around the line to detect light bites. When you feel a peck-pecking sensation, immediately release your finger from the line so the perch will be able to run with it. The fish won't feel any resistance because the line will travel freely through the sliding sinker lying on the bottom.

Count to about six before engaging the reel and attempting to set the hook. If you miss the fish, count to eight the next time you get a bite, then ten.

There also are a wide variety of artificial lures that will catch perch such as small spinners, $\frac{1}{8}$ ounce slim-minnow plugs, and wobbling spoons. I've consistently found the best to be those which imitate small minnows and are in representative baitfish colors—silver-gray, white, and gold. But without question the very best artificial is a tiny crappie jig about the size of a pencil eraser and weighing $\frac{3}{16}$ ounce. The fish seem to prefer white, yellow, or pink, as those colors simulate minnows, or a combination of orange and brown which simulates crayfish. A tiny fluff of marabou feathers on the hook is an added attraction, as the feathers pulse in the water, imparting the offering with a "breathing" effect that is an excellent strike-trigger.

Most times, I rely upon jigs when I've found a large school of perch and the action is so fast I don't want to waste time repeatedly baiting a hook. If the water is more than five or six feet deep, and you've been Lindy-rigging perch directly beneath the boat, switching to artificials doesn't mean you now have to begin casting. Just pay out line until you feel the jig, plug, or spoon bump bottom and then begin gently imparting it with life by jiggling your rod tip.

About the only time it's necessary to cast artificial lures for perch is when the water is less than five feet deep and the dark silhouette of a boat looming directly overhead would probably spook the fish. Other instances in which casting is recommended is when the perch are hugging the edges of shoreline weed cover and it's necessary to cast accurately to avoid too many hang-ups.

Incidentally, it's worth mentioning that schools of perch are like nomads that may be actively feeding in one place but an hour later

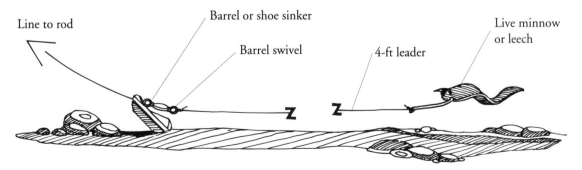

Assemble your Lindy-rig in this manner. The heart of the system is a sliding sinker that prevents the fish from detecting resistance when it picks up a bait being trolled across the bottom.

Lindy-rigging is commonly done with the outboard run in reverse to slow the boat's speed to a crawl.

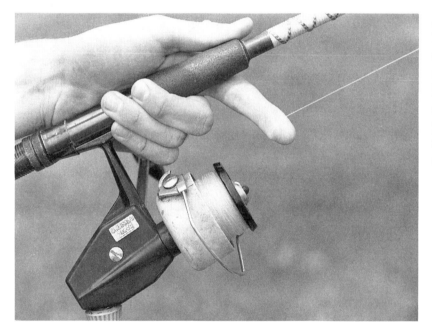

An open-face spinning reel is best for Lindy-rigging. Instead of engaging the bail, curl your finger around the line. When a perch bites, immediately release the line and pay out slack for a few moments before attempting to set the hook.

be a hundred yards away. To prevent losing contact with the school, many anglers attach the first perch they catch to a short length of line with a balloon at the other end and then release the fish. It will immediately return to its school, and the balloon bobbing along on the surface will provide a ready visual marker indicating the school's location as it randomly travels around.

PARTY BOAT FISHING

Another way to enjoy fun with perch is to corral several pals and spend an afternoon on a "head

The most renowned perch fishing is in the vicinity of the numerous islands and submerged reefs in Lake Erie's western basin.

boat." This type of perch fishing is extremely popular on the largest inland bodies of water such as Lake Erie, Lake Michigan, and others in the upper midwestern states where perch populations exist in great numbers.

Charter captains advertise in local newspapers and tabloids distributed by tourism agencies. Their rates are quite inexpensive, usually in the neighborhood of $15 per person, and this usually includes the bait. All you have to bring is your rod and perhaps sandwiches and drinks.

The charter boats we're describing here are safe, seaworthy craft that typically transport a load of twenty-five to fifty fishermen to well-known perch fishing grounds. This is the ultimate in perch fishing fun because of the convivial atmosphere that prevails, so bring your good mood and be prepared to catch scads of fish.

The fishing technique itself is rather universal. Everyone selects a position around the sides of the boat and, once the craft is anchored, the captain gives the go-ahead signal. You then pay out line until you feel your minnow bait hit bottom. Then you turn the reel handle just one revolution to raise the bait slightly off the bottom. The water may be as much as thirty feet deep, so bring an ample supply of split-shot sinkers and experiment to determine how much weight is needed.

To double your fishing fun, try using a wire spreader, sold for a buck in any tackleshop near popular perch fishing. This gizmo, which looks somewhat like the upper half of a coat hanger, is tied to the end of your line. From the two extended arms hang short dropper lines tied to hooks so you can fish two minnows simultaneously. When the perch are going crazy it's very common to catch two fish at the same time, and if each decides to go in a different direction you'll momentarily have your hands full!

However, catching "doubles" in this manner requires learning a little trick. When you feel a strike, set the hook with a gentle upward flick of your rod tip but don't begin to reel the fish in immediately. Simply maintain a tight line so the fish doesn't get off, let it swim around a bit, and invariably within less than ten seconds another perch will hit the second bait.

On the very same bodies of water where party boat fishing is popular, yet another splendid opportunity exists for catching yellow perch. This fishing takes place on the

On many large lakes, Lake Erie included, most perch anglers pay a modest fee to fish onboard a head boat. Quite often, hundreds of fish are caught in a single afternoon.

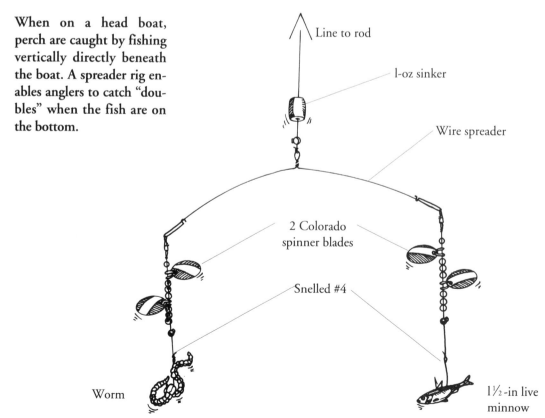

When on a head boat, perch are caught by fishing vertically directly beneath the boat. A spreader rig enables anglers to catch "doubles" when the fish are on the bottom.

Line to rod

l-oz sinker

Wire spreader

2 Colorado spinner blades

Snelled #4

Worm

1½-in live minnow

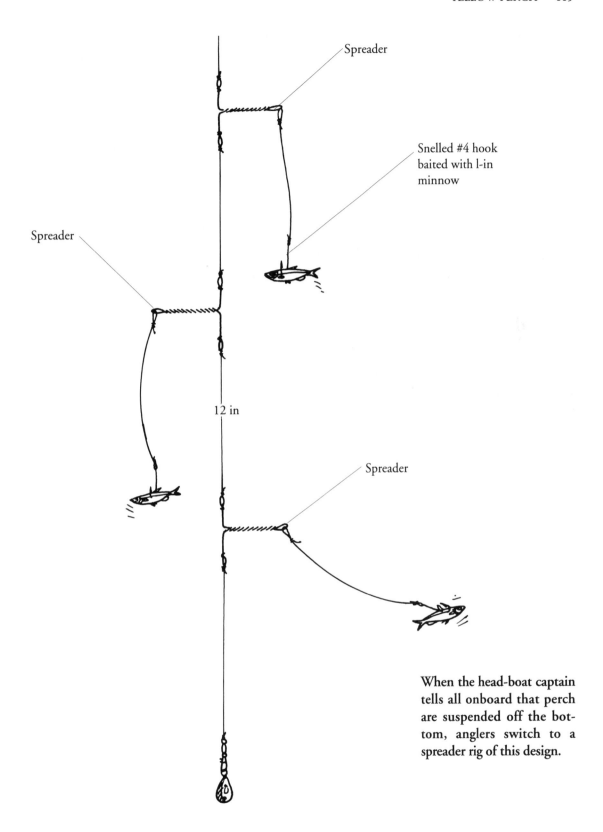

Spreader

Snelled #4 hook
baited with l-in
minnow

Spreader

12 in

Spreader

When the head-boat captain
tells all onboard that perch
are suspended off the bottom, anglers switch to a
spreader rig of this design.

On Lakes Erie, Huron, Ontario, and Michigan, exciting perch angling can be enjoyed by fishing from any of the many jetties and piers that jut into the water.

long piers, breakwater walls, and jetties that jut out into the lake and often are lined with dozens of anglers.

Since such concrete structures generally are constructed on top of manmade spans of slab rock and rubble for the purpose of protecting adjacent marinas and the mouths of feeder tributaries from incoming wave action, they are just like lengthy shoreline points in a smaller body of water and similarly attract perch year-round.

If the water depth immediately off the side of the breakwater wall or pier is six feet deep or more, you can drop a wire spreader baited with live minnows. If the water is relatively shallow close to the structure, try using one of the long, telescoping panfish poles described in Chapter 2 which will enable you to reach out 15 feet. Still another option is casting small slim-minnow lures or jigs dressed with plastic twister tails.

Biologists call the species *Perca flavescens,* which is Latin for "flavorful perch," but most anglers call the fish just plain fun. This season, why not find out for yourself?

10

Chain Pickerel

I once heard a fisherman describe a chain pickerel as a stick of dynamite looking for a place to explode, and that pretty well sums up the personality of this predatory water wolf.

The chain pickerel (*Esox niger*) is but a vest-pocket edition of the *Esox* clan, which also includes *Esox lucius* (the northern pike) and *Esox masquinongy* (the muskie). Upon occasion, chain pickerel grow to 4 or 5 pounds in weight, and the world record, taken in Georgia in 1961, weighed 9 pounds. But since the average chain pickerel you're likely to catch will undoubtedly weigh less than 2 pounds, most anglers refer to the much larger *Esox* specimens as gamefish and the chain pickerel as a panfish.

The "dynamite" reference is also very appropriate because you seldom know what to expect from a pickerel.

I remember one pickerel that came darting out of a weedbed and literally skittered and slashed along the surface for five yards in an attempt to catch up with my slim-minnow plug. When it finally connected, it immediately came out of the water about five or six times in rapid succession, shaking its head and tail-walking across the glassy surface.

Sometimes a pickerel takes a lure rather gingerly and then rolls on its side, comes to the surface and allows itself to be reeled in. But then, when it sees the boat, it makes an explosive bid for freedom and often snaps the short length of line.

Fishermen commonly mistake chain pickerel for small northern pike, especially in those waters where both species live, but there are easy ways to tell them apart. Pike generally have a flatter, spade-shaped head and their sides are splattered with large cream-colored spots. Chain pickerel, on the other hand, have a more elongated, pointed snout with black, chainlike markings along their sides.

Common nicknames for chain pickerel include *chainsides, jacks,* and *jackfish.*

The easiest way to envision the range of the chain pickerel is to draw a vertical line from central Minnesota to the southernmost tip of Texas. Everything to the east of that line is home to the chain pickerel, with its stronghold being the states along the eastern seaboard.

Chain pickerel are unpredictable fighters that often explode at boatside.

Chain pickerel are closely related to northern pike and muskies but usually weigh only 2 pounds on average. Their chainlike markings readily identify them.

No matter where the species is found, however, it has a distinct preference for very shallow water, seldom venturing deeper than eight feet during the open-water months. Look for it in tidal ponds, sloughs, backwater areas of larger lakes and reservoirs, cattail infested marshes in the headwaters regions of lakes, narrow tributary arms of large rivers, flooded swamps, cranberry bogs, and

Chain pickerel prefer shallow water and like to hang around weedbeds and lily pads. During the spring spawning periods, they often can be found in water only inches deep.

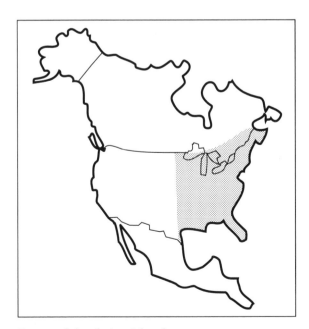

Range of the chain pickerel.

even narrow drainage ditches and canals.

Moreover, in any of these types of shallow habitat, chain pickerel prefer weeds, lily pads, and other vegetation to any other cover. In the absence of weeds during very early spring and late fall, look for the fish in standing timber and around drowned logs lying on the bottom. The fish also have a special liking for amber or slightly coffee-colored water.

Chain pickerel are carnivores of the highest order. Their favorite prey includes small fish (minnows, young panfish, and fingerling gamefish), crayfish, frogs and tadpoles, lizards, mice, birds, or any other living creature it thinks it can swallow.

HOW TO CATCH CHAIN PICKEREL

Chain pickerel are active feeders throughout the year, and since they remain in relatively shallow areas year around, finding and catching them is not difficult.

In early spring the fish move into thin water to mate, sometimes spawning at depth levels which can be measured in inches rather than feet. When spawning is concluded, the fish merely scoot away from the bank to find weedy cover. For the remaining months of the year, each individual may live and loaf within a confined area of a half-acre or less.

KEEPING LURE IN STRIKE ZONE

WRONG

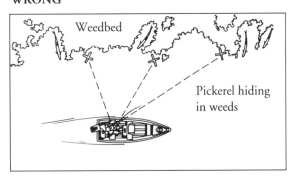

RIGHT

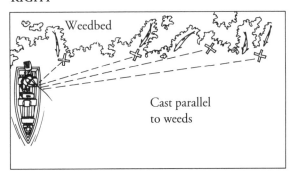

During the summer months, chain pickerel move into the thickest weeds they can find and keeping lures in the strike zone is important. Fish parallel to weedbeds whenever possible.

CASTING INTO A POTHOLE

WRONG

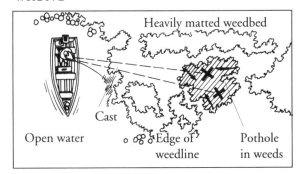

RIGHT

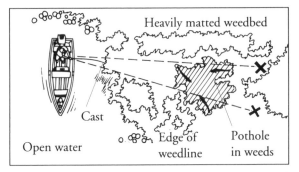

When fishing a pothole far back in matted weed growth, don't cast lures directly into the hole or you'll spook nearby pickerel. Cast beyond the hole and retrieve lure into the opening.

Popular artificial lures for chain pickerel include ¼ ounce balsa plugs, straight shaft spinners, spinnerbaits, and spoons, all of which represent small baitfish and minnows. I like such lures to be in contrasting baitfish colors such as yellow/green, white/ green, or silver/blue. The two hues present a flashing appearance in the stained and off-color water pickerel like best.

In fishing such lures, there is one important thing to keep in mind. If it's really hungry, the chain pickerel is a track star capable of making wind sprints to catch almost any bait or lure. But given a choice in the matter, it would prefer not to. It would rather play the role of mugger, hiding in some dark alley and dashing out to grab its victim.

Therefore, the angler who is able to keep his lure in the fish zone for the greatest length of time will invariably catch the most pickerel. An efficient way to do this when fishing heavily matted weedbeds is to maneuver your boat in close to the cover and cast parallel to the weeds; then with your rod tip work the lure back along the edge.

One type of hotspot I especially like to fish is narrow slots or trails that go far back through dense fields of weeds. Position your boat right at the mouth of the alley, make a long cast into the trail, and then retrieve the offering as close as possible to the left edge. Then make a second cast and retrieve the lure along the right edge.

I also like to fish open potholes in densely matted vegetation. But don't cast right into the pothole or the lure splashing down will probably spook a pickerel that is watching the opening from nearby. Instead, cast about six feet beyond the hole with a weedless spoon or small spinnerbait. When the lure splats down on top of the weed canopy, raise your rod tip to the 11 o'clock position, reel the slack out of the line, and then slowly crawl the lure across the top of the weeds and let it gently swim into the pothole opening. Be prepared to set the hook quickly. Then keep the fish's head up and muscle him out of the hole and right across the top of the weeds to open water; otherwise, he'll quickly tangle in the lettuce and break you off.

For this kind of work, medium-weight baitcasting tackle and 12-pound-test line gets the nod. However, when fishing the outside edges of weedbeds, I switch to open-face spinning tackle and 8-pound-test line.

Incidentally, when weed growth is sparse and pickerel are near standing timber and logs, it's again wise to avoid casting right to the intended

On lakes where weed growth is sparse, the chain pickerel's next favored hideout is brush and logs.

An effective way of catching chain pickerel hanging around submerged vegetation in open-lake areas is drift-fishing with live baits. But don't strike the instant your bobber ducks under!

target. Instead, cast far beyond the tree or log, begin the retrieve, and then manipulate the rod tip to the right or left to bring the lure within scant inches of the cover.

Many anglers like to fish live baits for chain pickerel. The best choice is a frisky minnow about 3 inches in length. Hook the minnow lightly through the lips with a size 4 or size 6 hook so it can swim around, place a single split-shot on the line above to keep the minnow from swimming to the surface, and use the adjustable slip-bobber rig described in Chapter 2.

The ideal time to fish live minnows with slip-bobbers is early in the season after spawning is concluded and weeds are still two or three feet beneath the surface. Chain pickerel like to lie hidden within the densest patches of weeds, or next to logs or stumps on the bottom, watching for prey that may venture within striking range.

Since chain pickerel are not schooling fish, they can be scattered widely, so that an angler will pick up one fish here and another somewhere else. Therefore, an excellent way to fish early-season submergent weeds or stump flats is to motor your boat to the lee side of a large shallow embayment, swampy area, or slough and then drift slowly with the wind to the other

side with your live minnow swimming along behind. Once you've reached the other side, motor back to the lee side again and try another drift, this time from a slightly different starting point to cover new water.

Here's what to be on the alert for when a chain pickerel rises to investigate your bait. First you'll see the bobber dancing around in a 3-foot circle. This is your minnow beginning to get scared. When the pickerel strikes, the bobber will go straight down about a foot and then angle off as the pickerel races away with the bait. Don't strike yet!

A chain pickerel takes a live minnow in its mouth sideways and after a short run comes to a stop, turns the minnow around in its mouth, and swallows it head-first. As a result, if you were to strike the very instant the bobber ducked under, the hook wouldn't yet be in position and you'd probably pull the bait from the fish's mouth.

So as soon as you see the bobber beginning to dance, open the bail on your spinning reel so the pickerel can run off with some free line without feeling resistance. As soon as you can tell that the running fish has stopped and is no longer taking line, you can presume it is in the process of turning the minnow to swallow it. Give it a five-count, close the bail of your reel, then strike to set the hook.

To counter the last-ditch fight of chain pickerel, I like to vary the drag setting on my reel. I keep the drag screwed down tight while casting, so it won't slip when I set the hook and so I can strong-arm a fish out of heavy cover. But as the fish comes closer to the boat I begin releasing the drag. When it's within ten feet of the boat I release the drag altogether and place my thumb on the baitcasting reel spool, or, in the case of a spin-ning reel, my index finger on the flange of the spool. The advantage of this is to counter the thrashing last-minute run a pickerel often makes at boatside.

Just like their larger pike and muskie cousins, chain pickerel have sharp teeth that can easily sever your line if precautions are not taken. But I don't like to use wire leaders because they impede the action of smaller lures and minnows used for chain pickerel. So I always use a shock-tippet instead, a 3-foot length of 15-pound-test abrasion-resistant mono.

11

Yellow Bass

The yellow bass, *Morone mississippiensis,* is sometimes also referred to as a *barfish* or *striped bass,* or simply *stripe.* By whatever moniker, however, it is biologically classified as a "temperate" or "true" bass, which makes it very closely related to the white bass, striped bass, and hybrid bass. Some anglers claim the yellow bass, with its firm, white, flaky flesh is nearly as delicious as the yellow perch.

The yellow bass often is confused with the white bass. The two look nearly identical in body conformation and size, but there are telltale differences. The yellow bass has a slightly yellow tinge to its otherwise platinum-colored sides, and its dark stripes, running from the gill flaps to the tail, are more pronounced. Further, the white bass has a small tooth patch on the tongue; the yellow bass does not.

Adult yellow bass average ¾ pound in weight and perhaps 11 inches in length. The world record, from Indiana, weighed slightly more than 2 pounds.

Yellow bass are closely related to striped bass and provide excellent eating.

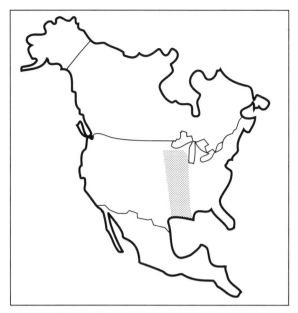

Range of the yellow bass.

The species has an elongated range found within the central portion of the United States, stretching from Minnesota to Louisiana and eastern Texas. Attempts to expand this range have been only marginally successful in spotty locales. The reason is believed to be a result of the species' habitat preferences. It thrives in lakes, reservoirs, and the larger river systems but must have access to very shallow reefs and gravel bars. Another way the yellow bass differs from its lookalike cousin the white bass is that the white customarily prefers to spawn in feeder tributaries whereas the yellow bass generally prefers open lakes.

A characteristic shared by all members of the temperate bass family is that once they've grown beyond the fry and fingerling stage, for the remainder of their lives they feed almost exclusively upon shad and other baitfish. A popular method of catching the species in the spring, when the water temperature is in the high sixties, is to use a bottom-contour map and depth sounder to locate shallow gravel bars in mid-lake regions, then cast small minnow-shaped plugs and spinners over and around the structures.

When spawning is concluded, yellow bass exhibit the same type of nomadic behavior as white bass: they gather in large schools and continually roam in search of pods of minnows and other small baitfish. Yet there are two ways in which their feeding habits differ from those of white bass. First, while it's common for white bass to slash into their forage on the surface, yellow bass are predominantly bottom feeders or mid-depth feeders, rarely causing a visible surface commotion to attract the notice of anglers. Second, during the early and late hours of the day, yellow bass frequently venture into very shallow water to disperse and feed.

FISHING METHODS

Like white bass, yellow bass travel along well-defined bottom structures such as an old riverbed winding along the lake floor or a lengthy drop-off, and it's sometimes possible to determine their morning and evening feeding locations in the shallows. Simply study your map, searching for places where the old river bed loops in close to the shoreline or where an underwater drop-off yields to expansive shallow flats. If these shallow shoreline areas have downed timber, logs, or brush cover, all the better.

During the late spring, summer, and fall, a popular way of finding yellow bass at midday is by trolling the lengths of drop-offs and the edges of the old river channel. Minnow-type plugs, spoons, and straight-shaft spinners are good bets now, in small sizes (no more than 2 inches in length) and in representative baitfish colors.

To get these lures down to the levels at which yellow bass are likely to be found, many anglers rely upon the venerable Wolf River Rig. To make one, tie the terminal end of your line to one of the eyes of a three-way swivel. Then tie an 18-inch dropper line with a 1-ounce sinker on the end to another eye of the swivel. Finally, tie a 36-inch drop-back line to the third eye of

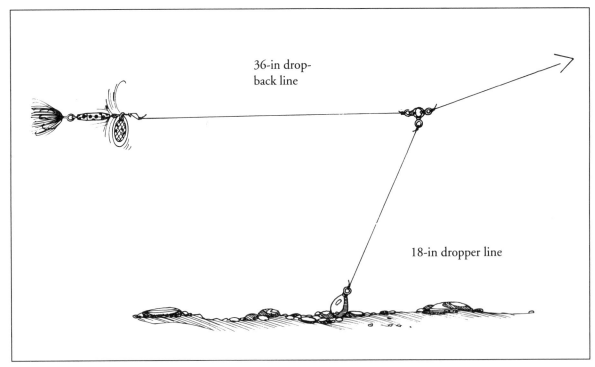

Yellow bass are predominantly bottom-feeders. The best way to catch them during summer and fall is by using a Wolf River Rig.

the swivel, and tie the lure to the end. When trolling slowly, you should be able to feel the sinker bump bottom occasionally; if not, go to a slightly heavier weight.

Once a yellow bass is caught, throw a marker buoy overboard to serve as a reference and then begin vertically pumping small jigs with plastic twister tails or jigging spoons and there's an excellent chance of catching still more fish. Or, if the school of yellow bass is on the move, simply use your depth sounder to continue trolling the length of the structure you were working.

When the fish periodically infiltrate the shallows, a wide variety of small plugs and spinners are effective. Yellow bass are not particularly fussy in this regard; if it looks like a minnow and swims like a minnow, they'll be inclined to believe it is a minnow and waste no time grabbing it.

However, in many regions, such as Tennessee's Reelfoot Lake, which is believed to possess the country's largest yellow bass population,

a popular shallow-water fishing technique is the same as we described for crappies in Chapter 6: use a 14-foot panfish pole, a stand-up bobber, and a small minnow impaled on a size 8 thin-wire hook and dabble the bait around the perimeters of brush piles, standing timber, stumps, and logs.

An alternative, if you get into plenty of fish and the action is too fast to bother with rebaiting hooks, is a slip-bobber rig with a small jig dressed with a curlytail grub, as described for spring perch fishing in Chapter 9.

Incidently, when trolling with a Wolf River Rig, I like medium-weight spinning tackle and 8-pound-test line. When venturing into the shallows to cast lightweight lures, I then pop out the spool of 8-pound line and snap into place a second spool filled with 4- or 6-pound line. When using a long fiberglass panfish pole, it is necessary to use at least 15-pound line to straighten the hook when pulling free of snags.

12

White Perch

The white perch is not a perch at all but yet another member of the temperate bass family and therefore closely related to the white bass and yellow bass. In fact, it looks almost identical to both fish, except that it has coarser scales, a pale-green/silvery coloration, and lacks stripes on its sides.

Biologists call the species *Morone americana* and it is the only panfish I'm aware of that does not have a host of nicknames.

Perhaps this is because of its very restricted range along the eastern coastline from Nova Scotia to the southernmost tip of South Carolina.

Although the white perch has gradually infiltrated still other waters as far inland as Lake Erie, it is predominantly an inhabitant of brackish rivers that drain into the ocean, or estuaries,

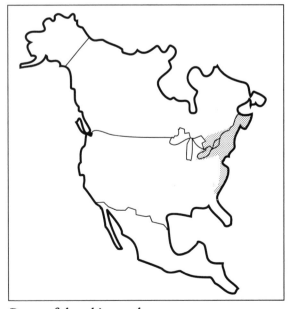

Range of the white perch.

White perch prefer brackish rivers that drain into the ocean, or estuaries and ponds that eventually connect with the sea.

ponds, and lake systems that in some way or another eventually connect with the sea. The species even prowls around in shallow ocean areas just offshore, but few saltwater anglers fish for them.

Adult white perch average a pound in weight and 10 to 12 inches in length, although 2-pounders are not uncommon. The world record, from Maine, was a 4-pound-plus goliath. Many anglers consider the white perch one of the finest food fishes, and it is a spirited fighter when taken on light tackle.

Spring spawning action gets underway as soon as the water temperature reaches 50 degrees, but the species is rather haphazard in its mating activities. Unpaired males and females swarm upstream into shallow coastal rivers or lake tributaries, randomly disperse their eggs and milt, then over the course of many weeks

begin drifting back toward deeper water. The fact that white perch are so prolific despite such careless mating behavior is probably due to the extensive numbers of eggs produced by the females; a given adult female scatters as many as 150,000 eggs as she slowly swims about in shallow shoreline areas.

FISHING METHODS

In the spring, white perch feed heavily upon shrimp, crabs, and insect larvae in muddy bottom areas. Since such foods can be difficult to gather or buy in baitshops, anglers traditionally rely upon worms.

The customary tackle for this kind of work is light spinning gear and 4- or 6-pound test line. To the terminal end of the line, tie on a size 8

In the spring, white perch migrate far up rivers to spawn. Yet they periodically stop in the vicinity of wing dams, quiet eddies, and bridge abutments to feed. Keep traveling upstream until you locate such fish-holding structures.

hook, and slightly above it clamp a split-shot to take the bait down. Or use a slip-bobber rig, adjusting the float so the bait is not more than a few inches above the bottom. Small jigs weighing ³⁄₃₂ ounce, in brown, black, or orange, slowly hopped along the bottom with ultralight spinning or spincast tackle also account for their share of fish, as do straight-shaft spinners with a small piece of worm impaled upon the hook.

The intriguing thing about spring fishing for white perch is that it is a "feast or famine" type of angling in which it often is necessary to move around quite a lot and test-fish many different areas in an attempt to find places where the fish are congregating. Yet once they have been located, it's common to catch fifty or sixty in only an hour's time.

One sure tip-off that white perch action is taking place is noting the presence of many other anglers lining specific stretches along a riverbank. Otherwise, pay particular attention to the tailraces just below dams (which prevent the fish from swimming farther upstream), bridge abutments and wing dams (which afford resting places protected from the current), and quiet eddies and pockets along the shorelines.

Once spawning is completed and the water temperature rises into the mid-60s, the summer fishing period gets underway and it is generally the most exciting of the year. By now the fish have gradually moved out of the shallow spawning areas and back into the river proper or the main lake.

At this time, when they are in rivers, they especially like to hang around shallow sandbars, gravel shoals, and the edges of weedlines and

On quiet, midsummer evenings, white perch commonly slurp insects off the surface just like trout. Any dry fly, light or dark, should produce well.

brushy cover where they continue to grub for bottom-dwelling aquatic life. So the same angling tactics that produced earlier during the spawning period are likewise effective now; it's just that it takes place progressively farther downstream.

In lakes and reservoirs the fish likewise prefer to summer on bars, shoals, and windswept gravel shorelines but at substantially greater depths, sometimes twenty feet or more, and their diet now also includes small minnows and baitfish.

When fishing lakes or large ponds, many anglers like to troll or drift-fish slowly with straight-shaft spinners adorned with worms, using the same Wolf River Rig described for yellow bass. Random fish are caught by this method, but it's really only a means of biding time until faster action begins. It's common for white perch to corral minnow schools against the surface similar to the way white bass charge into surface-swimming schools of baitfish. This most often occurs during the flat-water periods of dawn and dusk. When anglers spot this action, they move to within cautious casting distance and throw slim minnow plugs and other representative baitfish lures.

Yet another exciting form of white perch fishing during midsummer is that which frequently occurs during the evening hours when the fish dimple the surface as they feed upon various types of insects, especially mayflies. There is no mistaking this feeding activity because hundreds of intermittent pockmarks may disrupt the calm surface over an area spanning an acre or more.

Now is when the fly fisherman enjoys superb fishing by casting floating patterns. Don't worry if you're not an entomologist capable of identifying the specific species of insect being fed upon because almost any dry fly, light or dark, tied on a size 10 hook will be greedily engulfed by a white perch.

13

River Tactics

Like their counterparts in lakes and reservoirs, panfish in rivers also hang out near weeds, rocks, woody cover such as stumps, and irregular bottom contours. But there is one additional condition that greatly influences their lives and that is *current*.

The flow of water that constitutes a current has certain characteristics, regardless of where in the country the river or stream is located. For one, a current is always stronger just below a dam or rapids and for a few miles downstream, until it gradually begins to diminish in velocity. Also, any flow of moving water always takes the easiest route to lower elevations, in a straight line, until some land feature diverts it, creating a bend. In time, the current washes out and undercuts the outside bend, thereby making the water much deeper there. Conversely, the inside of the bend has a somewhat quieter flow of water, which allows sand, gravel, and sediment carried downstream by the current to settle to the bottom in such places and create a shallow bar or shoal. In flatland areas, a river or stream may be straight as an arrow for mile after mile. But in hilly or mountainous terrain, or in re-

gions where there are mixtures of very soft and hard ground, perhaps with occasional rock or shale deposits, the river will predictably take on a serpentine form.

As a general rule, the current of any flowing waterway will usually be much stronger toward the surface and toward the middle of the flow. Reduced current velocity is usually found along the floor of the river and close to the banks. In smaller rivers, various panfish species commonly take advantage of this situation by resting in depressions scooped out of the bottom, letting the fast water rush above them. Or they may rest behind the protection of midstream boulders or along the shoreline where cover formations create pockets of less turbulent water. In larger rivers, panfish also seek refuge away from strong current by holding on the down-current sides of islands, near wing-dams, or in and around such shoreline cover as trees, logs, rocks, and stumps.

But above all, the most important thing to keep in mind about current is that none of the panfish species likes to spend much time in swift water but prefers to rest in quieter currents directly adjacent to the main flow. And they will always face into the current, as this allows them to maintain their positions with the least expenditure of energy. It also allows them to keep on the watch for food which the rushing current may bring their way. They may have to dart out momentarily into the fast water to capture prey, but very shortly they will return to their holding stations in the quieter edge waters.

FINDING PANFISH IN LARGE RIVERS

Panfish in large rivers usually prefer the shorelines and feeder tributaries to the main channel, which is generally too deep and swift, and devoid of cover. Indeed, the bottom is likely to have been scoured clean by dredges to facilitate barge and tugboat traffic.

One exception to this rule applies to those particular panfish species—white bass, in particular—which gang up in large schools during midsummer and prowl open water to feed upon surface-swimming schools of baitfish, in which case use the same tactics described in Chapter 7.

Otherwise, no matter which panfish species are the target of the day, I invariably concentrate my efforts along shoreline shelves. These features, quite common on rivers used for interstate commerce, appear as narrow benches extending out from the bank perhaps twenty yards before dropping off sharply into the main river channel. They're quite attractive to all panfish species because of a combination of desirable features, such as a suitable water depth ranging from two to fifteen feet and an abundance of log jams, driftwood, stumps, boulders, and similar cover. Also, although we noted earlier that rivers generally do not have an overly abundant food base, at least not compared to reservoirs, what food there is in large rivers is concentrated in the shallow littoral zone of shoreline shelves as described above.

Another feature of many large rivers that can afford a wealth of panfishing excitement is an oxbow. This is a place where a loop or S-turn in the river channel has been straightened out by dredges to facilitate barge traffic. The result is the formation of a crescent-shaped backwater almost like a small lake. Most times, there will be a narrow cut leading into the oxbow from the main river channel, and another cut exiting, but during low water periods these can be reduced to bare trickles. Never-

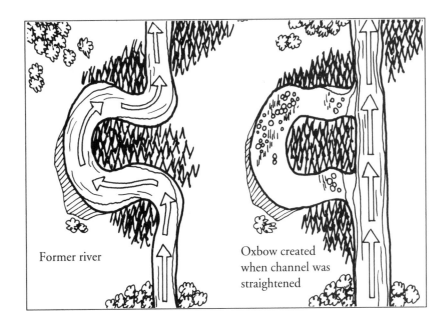

Former river

Oxbow created when channel was straightened

An oxbow in a river is a good place to find all species of panfish because it simulates the exact conditions found in a lake.

Wing dams play important roles in the lives of fish in those rivers where current velocity fluctuates.

theless, the distinct absence of current, along with the large quantities of brush, logs, and weeds that typically choke these oxbows, make for optimal panfish habitat that can be fished in the same manner as one might work the embayment of any lake or reservoir.

In large rivers another location for finding panfish are the wingdams just downstream from dams or locks. These are manmade structures of cribbing and natural materials, either gravel with a cement binder or logs and railroad ties interspersed with boulders, and their function is to shunt the main flow of the current toward the middle of the river, thus preventing the banks from seriously eroding. When the current is slack, fish may be on the upstream side of the wingdam, but if it is moderate to heavy they will always be on the protected downstream side.

Of all big-river features, however, the most attractive to panfish are the numerous tributaries feeding into the main river channel. Invariably, the shorelines of such creeks and small rivers are lined with trees, stumps, rocks, weedbeds, and other favored panfish cover. And since such tributaries are never dredged, the bottom may have holes, bars, rock piles,

In large rivers, key locations for finding all panfish species are the numerous feeder tributaries that eventually dump into the main channel.

and similar fish-attracting structures commonly found in lakes and reservoirs.

A prime time of year to fish feeder tributaries

is during the spring, when all panfish are inclined to leave the banks of the main river channel where they've spent the winter months. They instinctively enter tributaries and travel upstream into quieter, shallower water to spawn. Some species such as white bass and perch may travel far up these tributaries looking for secondary feeder tributaries, but generally it's the first mile or two of the primary tributary that proves the most productive for all panfish.

As summer approaches, the fish begin to drift back toward the banks of the main river channel and disperse along shoreline shelves, although a high percentage of many species such as bluegills, sunfish, and crappies can be counted to remain in the tributary itself.

About the time of the first hard frost in fall, those panfish species which left the primary tributaries to take up locations along the banks of the main river channel migrate back into the feeder tributaries again, but they don't travel as far upstream as they did in the spring. Instead, in the first several hundred yards or so, near the tributary mouth, they go on feeding rampages in preparation for winter. North of the Mason-Dixon line, this is a time of year when there are large shad die-offs in rivers, and this creates splendid opportunities for catching panfish that feed on small minnows (crappies, perch, white bass).

The seasonal keys to unlocking successful big-river panfishing can therefore be summarized as follows: During the spring, concentrate upon the feeder tributaries; during the summer, work both the tributaries and shorelines adjacent to the main river channel; and during the fall, go back to the tributaries, but work only the mouths. Furthermore, during all seasons, capitalize upon any opportunities to fish wingdams just below locks and dams and especially oxbows.

Small streams and rivers are challenging, especially if they are shallow, clear, and possess thick shoreline cover. Accurate casting now determines one's success.

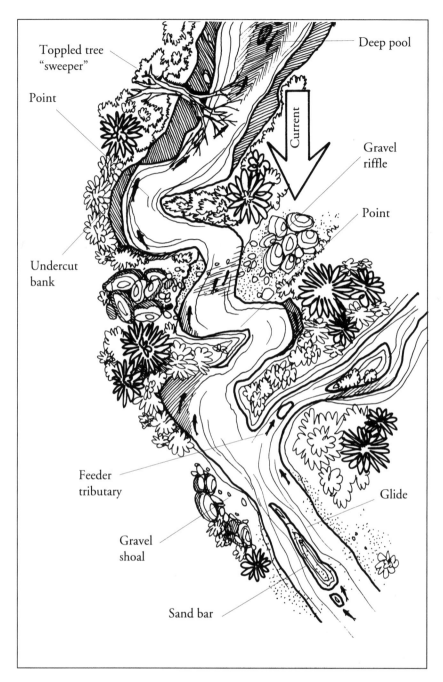

Toppled tree "sweeper"

Point

Undercut bank

Deep pool

Current

Gravel riffle

Point

Feeder tributary

Gravel shoal

Glide

Sand bar

In small rivers and streams, the current gouges the landscape and creates many diverse structures. The most attractive to panfish include undercut banks, riffles, glides, points, shoals, and locations where trees have toppled into the water.

STREAM SAVVY

Very small rivers offer both the easiest and yet the most challenging panfishing imaginable. On the one hand, an angler with even the most rudimentary knowledge of fish behavior can look at a small stream and immediately make educated guesses as to where fish are likely to be holding. But trying to catch them may be altogether another matter. The water always seems to be moving too fast, or it's so shallow the fish are spooky, or the most attractive holding stations are jailed by impregnable cover.

In such shallow habitats, panfish do not gather in schools. There may be exceptions in which widely separated deep pools hold loose groupings of fish during the midsummer and winter months, but in the great majority of cases the fish are loners.

All streams and creeks—whether they meander through rural farmlands, black-bottom swamps, woodland tracts, or deep rocky gorges—share some traits. For one, like all flowing waters, they always take the path of least resistance, carving their way through soft-soil regions, diverting right or left to skirt hardpan, which gives each the appearance of a serpent twisting across the landscape. Streams also vary widely in their bottom contours, for as the water flows to lower elevations it sluices over soft soil and hard, creating an undulating effect in a series of deep pools, bars, shallow riffles, and long glides.

North of the Mason-Dixon line, rock bass, white bass, bluegills, redear sunfish, and green sunfish inhabit most small streams. Throughout the South, the predominant residents are bluegills, warmouth, green sunfish, redbreast sunfish, redear sunfish, and white bass.

The best all-around outfit is a 5-foot, 2-ounce spinning rod married to a small open-face reel. On occasion, spincasting and ultralight baitcasting tackle may be justified, and there may be myriad opportunities to use flycasting tackle, but open-face spinning reels are by far the most versatile. With this gear you can quickly snap into place interchangeable spools of line to meet given conditions. I usually rely upon 6-pound test most of the day, but whenever I come to a crystal-clear pool of quiet water, I like to switch to 4-pound. If there's a sluggish stretch full of logjams, weeds, or other cover, 8-pound test is called for.

Also, much of any stream or creek bank is lined with trees and overhanging branches, which gives the waterway a tunnel appearance. Moreover, along the shorelines, particularly where there are sharp bends in the creek, the outside turn will be deeply undercut and the root masses of the shoreline trees will be exposed and offer an infinite variety of hiding places for fish. To work these shorelines effectively, you often must cast from rather unorthodox positions, making use of underhand or sidearm throws, and in such situations spinning gear is far easier to handle than baitcasting, spincasting, or fly tackle.

In streams and creeks, panfish feed as avidly upon aquatic insect life as they do in large rivers, lakes, and reservoirs. Yet they also feed heavily upon grasshoppers and locusts blown

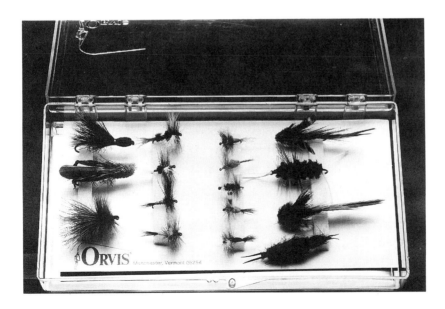

Panfish that live in streams dine upon a wide variety of insects, including grasshoppers and locusts. Flyrod lures that imitate these critters can pay off handsomely.

Should you fish upstream or down? Both can be productive. But in either case, when the water is very shallow, it's usually wise to disembark and wade-fish.

into the water from nearby fields or dislodged by the wind from overhead branches. So in addition to the usual supply of wet flies and nymphs, I sometimes like to cast somewhat larger flies such as the Muddler Minnow or a hand-tied grasshopper. Of course, with spinning tackle you have to use a clear plastic bubble for casting weight.

Panfish in streams and creeks also feed heavily upon tiny crayfish and hellgrammites, both of which can be simulated by small brown jigs with brown or dark-orange grub tails. And, unlike their brethren in larger waters, panfish in streams and creeks devour large quantities of pin minnows. These are tiny chubs and shiners no more than an inch in length, and they can be simulated by small silver-gray streamer flies and a wide variety of ⅛-ounce straight-shaft spinners.

The live bait angler should do well in streams with tiny crayfish, earthworms, or crickets.

UPSTREAM OR DOWN?

Anglers heatedly disagree about whether rivers should be fished upstream or down. There are advantages and disadvantages to both methods.

If you make a ruckus when fishing downstream, it is likely to have one of two effects: Gravel, silt, and other debris that you dislodge by wading or by carelessly maneuvering your craft through shallow riffles will wash downstream through places you intend to fish next and may spook the fish. Other times, though, I've seen just the opposite occur. You may inadvertently kick up crustaceans, nymphs, and other tasty tidbits which drift downstream and incite panfish to start feeding on goodies that come their way—including your lures.

Whenever possible, however, I like to fish upstream, occasionally making use of a small outboard or electric motor if the current is just a bit too fast for leisurely paddling. The main reason for this preference is that panfish face into the current, not only to maintain their positions with the least expenditure of energy but also to watch for drifting food. Thus lures or bait drifting downstream appear perfectly natural.

If fishing downstream is the only practical way to work the water, I'd like to make several suggestions. First, stay in your craft as much as possible. And rather than casting directly downstream, hug whichever bank appears to be featureless and without much cover (and likely holds few if any fish) and cast in a quartering upstream direction to work the opposite side.

To prevent your boat from grating on sand and gravel bars, you may have to disembark occasionally and wade quietly. In some quiet sections of water, you can sling the craft's bow rope over your shoulder and the boat will follow behind you, enabling you to sneak unobtrusively to within casting range of suspected panfish lairs. Yet if there's much current, this tactic can cause endless frustration, as the boat will continually prod your backside or get ahead of you. Then I beach my canoe or johnboat temporarily and hike along some gravel bar in a crouched position, casting into shoreline pockets and around various midstream obstructions. After the water has been thoroughly fished, I retrieve my craft and venture on downstream to the next likely location.

READING THE WATER

For any species of panfish inhabiting small rivers, streams and creeks, it is essential to learn how to analyze the various components that make up the waterway. Each pool, glide, and riffle presents an entirely different picture puzzle which must be carefully evaluated. The current may slide from one side to the other, submerged rocks or logs with water rushing over the tops are sure to be present, and occasionally you'll come upon "sweepers," or toppled shoreline trees with their crowns lying in the water that stick out into the main flow.

As in larger rivers, the current in smaller waterways is always stronger near the surface and in midstream, and slower along the bottom, close to the banks, and directly behind obstructions. Panfish holding in midstream are the greatest challenge. Nearly always, they'll choose semiprotected pockets close to the main current flow (which carries most of the food), but *how* close depends upon the speed of the water and the particular species of fish.

For example, let's consider the situation near a large boulder in the middle of a creek. On the upstream side, the current is forced to split around the rock. Right where the current splits, particulate matter in suspension will have settled out and piled up, but directly behind the boulder there is almost invariably a depression. Assuming the current velocity is relatively mild, several rock bass or perch may be holding immediately in front of the boulder, and an appropriate lure such as a wet fly should be cast quartering upstream several yards ahead of where the current splits. The natural flow of the water will carry the lure around the boulder and into view of a fish holding in the quieter water behind. Approximately five or ten yards downstream of the rock, the two tendrils of diverted current join once again and the water appears bubbly or foam-flecked. If there is any unique bottom feature present at this junction, such as rubble, expect action.

Another hotspot for panfish is where two streams join, or where a small stream enters the main flow of a small river. Fresh water gushing into the main channel, especially after summer showers, acts like a tonic, and if you're there with anything resembling eats you're in business. These locations, at any time of year, often present a divided appearance where the cloudy or murky run-off water rushing in from the stream tributary yields to the clearer water of the main channel. This edge is a type of structure, and panfish often relate to it as religiously as they might to a weedline in a lake.

It's very common for small rivers to be so murky that you can't see below-surface rocks, logs, and other obstructions that may be serving as holding stations for fish. Here again is where learning how to read the water can pay off in handsome catches.

The trick is to take a few minutes to watch the surface of the water and any drifting bits of flotsam, twigs, leaves, or even foam. A sudden change in the direction of the moving debris can indicate what lies below. If a twig or leaf suddenly deviates to the left or right from its straight downstream drift, then something below, probably a rock or log, is diverting the current. If the debris seems to hesitate, or briefly scoots back upstream several yards, it is being influenced by swirling eddy water, which indicates a quiet pocket directly below and some obstruction on the bottom just a few yards upstream. Similarly, a large boil on the surface indicates a large underwater obstacle, such as slab rock.

Although, as mentioned earlier, I like to fish upstream whenever possible, working sweepers—shoreline trees toppled into the water—is an exception to the rule. I first learned how to fish them effectively from panfish guide Norris Wilcourt on an unnamed tributary of the Tennessee River.

Norris positioned our boat at an upstream vantage point and then slowly paid out line so the gentle current carried his straight-shaft spinner downstream right into the maze of tangled branches. By keeping slight tension on the line, he was able to keep the lure nosing into the current so it looked like a small minnow trying to maintain its position. After two minutes, Wilcourt paid out several more feet of line, allowing the lure to "drop back" farther into a slightly different holding pattern.

"There!" he said excitedly, striking back with a deep bend in his rod and quickly cranking the fish away from the cover before it had a chance to crochet the line through the latticework of limbs. It was a hefty redear sunfish, and then Norris proceeded to take three more of exactly the same size from the very same tree, proving the effectiveness of the drop-back technique. It's rather strange that panfish anglers have only recently begun using this super tactic, because Michigan steelhead fishermen have known it for generations.

Without question, the largest panfish come from sweepers located in the longest, deepest, and quietest pools. Generally, the fish will be holding right in the middle of the sweepers when the current is mild, dropping back to the far downstream side as the velocity periodically increases after a rainstorm.

READING THE WATER

BEND IN RIVER

1. Bend in river occurs when current veers away from hard terrain and takes path of easiest resistance. Washing effect of current eventually undercuts bank and forms long, deep pocket. Largest fish in this stretch will be beneath undercut outside bank, if water isn't too swift.

BRIDGE ABUTMENTS

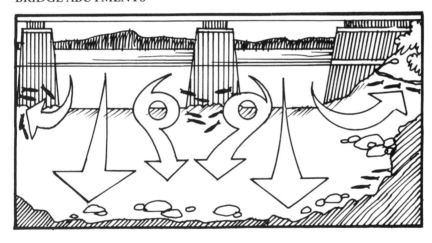

2. Bridge abutments interrupt flow of water in a river, which causes the formation of clam eddies, specifically to the holes they gouge in the riverbed. There, fish wait for the current to bring them food. Best bet for fishing such areas is to anchor downstream of the bridge abutments.

FALLEN TREE

3. Fallen tree extending into main current reduces flow of water and causes creation of a deep hole. Fish on downstream side of this obstruction have easy access to food washing down in main flow. Tree provides fish with protection from predators. Slow water enables them to preserve energy they'd normally use in fighting current.

BOULDER AND FEEDER STREAMS

4. Boulder in middle of river forces water to split and go around either side. Water's force often gouges a depression behind boulder. Fish will hold in the slower water of pocket and thus have easy access to any forage washing by in main flow. Feeder stream emptying into river gouges out a deep hole in the main channel. Fish like to hold either in the deep pool itself, or along its upstream edge.

DAMS

5. Dam across river is good fish-holding spot. Though fish are unable to fight the direct current coming through gates, they will hold just below the apron at base of dam. Riprap downstream of a dam also attracts fish.

RIFFLES

6. Riffles in stream seldom hold large fish because the water there is too shallow. White water coming out of riffles will dig out a hole, however, and that is where the fish will be, particularly around large obstructions such as boulders.

14

Ice Fishing

Finding panfish during the winter when a shroud of ice blankets the water is perhaps easier than at any other time of year. Just look for the other anglers!

Frostbite anglers are a gregarious, fun-loving lot. Moreover, they customarily catch far more fish than any other category of fishermen, and for good reason. With a large number of baits lowered through the ice, you can often hold a roving school of fish there for quite a long time—something that might be impossible to accomplish if only one angler were in the vicinity. Also, there are bound to be hot periods and slack times during almost any ice-angling foray, and what better way to kill time than by chit-chatting with other members of the fraternity?

If you're going it alone, though, finding panfish beneath the ice still is relatively easy. One key is learning how weed growth influences the lives of fish.

Various species of aquatic vegetation, of course, grow only in shallow to moderately deep water. Seldom are they found in water more than fifteen feet deep, simply because in most lakes sunlight cannot penetrate much deeper than that. As the sunlight bathes the weeds,

they engage in a food-making process known as photosynthesis, whereby they absorb carbon dioxide and other nutrients and in turn give off oxygen as a by-product.

Finding panfish beneath the ice is easy. Just look for the other anglers! Then, join the fun, because the more anglers present to dangle baits the better the chance of holding roving fish in that location.

Early in the winter season, spend most of your time fishing known weedbeds because they'll be releasing oxygen into the water. Later in the season, fish woody cover because weedbeds will be going dormant and releasing carbon dioxide.

During the spring and summer months, this life-sustaining oxygen is dispersed to all parts of the lake by wind and wave action, which thus homogenizes the water and allows panfish to roam at will and find their preferred forage. Yet, during the winter, the surface layer of ice prevents wind and subsequent wave action from dispersing the oxygen released from the weeds. Panfish therefore tend to cluster in high-oxygen regions where weeds are most prevalent.

It is not difficult to locate these weedy areas. You can probably recall certain coves, embayments, and shallow banks where weed growth was profuse during the open-water months. A good starting place is along the outer, deep-water edges of these weeds where the water will most probably be six to fifteen feet deep, or within large pockets or open spaces in wide expanses of weed growth.

However, it is imperative to keep in mind that what we have said so far applies *only* to the first month or so of the ice fishing season. As the ice steadily grows thicker, and occasionally finds itself blanketed with snow for long periods of time, there is a distinct reversal in the lake's ecosystem. Less sunlight now penetrates the ice, causing most vegetation to turn brown and fall into a dormant stage until the following spring.

When this happens, the weed growth begins decomposing and settling to the bottom. As it does so, it *consumes* oxygen and gives off carbon dioxide, making the immediate area far less attractive to all fish species.

So remember all the weedy places in your favorite lake and greet the ice fishing season by fishing exclusively near these known weedbeds. Weeks later, when your catch ratio begins to taper off, begin searching for other lake areas where weed growth is customarily absent.

Generally, the fish will have abandoned shallow, gradually sloping bottom contours (which were choked with weeds months earlier) and moved toward much steeper banks. Since most panfish species like to stay close to some kind of cover, and since weeds are now unattractive, the two alternatives most often sought are woody cover or rocky cover. Ready examples of woody cover include stumps, standing timber, drowned brush piles, logjams, and the crowns of trees that have toppled into the water.

If not much woody cover is in evidence, panfish commonly associate with a wide variety of bottom configurations such as old stream channels winding across the floor of the lake, the old riverbed itself, stairstep ledge formations along steep banks, drop-offs, sunken islands, deep sandbars, sheer rock walls along shorelines, and steep shoreline points littered with big slabs of rock. In many lakes, panfish also can be found along the rubble facings of dams and causeways and around the concrete pilings of bridges and railroad trestles that may span the lake. Many ice anglers use portable, flasher-type depth sounders to locate such features as sunken, rock-capped islands, sandbars, deep stump fields, sharp bends in stream channels on the lake floor, and the like.

You don't have to cut a hole through the ice to use your depth sounder. Simply brush away the snow with your glove, rub a tiny bit of antifreeze, from a small pocket vial, onto the bottom of the transducer and hold it flat against the smooth ice.

GEARING UP FOR ICE FISHING

Now that you're aware of general lake areas to begin plying your efforts, consider tackle and

On lakes where the ice is less than 10 inches thick, a homemade spud is adequate for cutting holes. Shown here is the author's ice-fishing sled, specifically designed to carry with ease all necessary tackle and other gear.

On northern lakes where ice may be several feet thick, an angler can cut numerous holes in minutes with a gasoline-powered auger.

related equipment. First, you'll need some way to cut holes through the ice. Many wintertime anglers use a special ice auger that you turn like a big hand drill. Sharp edges on the blade corkscrew down through the ice in brief minutes. Quality ice augers cost $100; they last a lifetime and are available through fishing catalogs and at tackleshops near popular ice fishing lakes.

More expensive ice augers have gas motors attached to them. Prices run as high as $400, but they will chew through two feet of ice in seconds and are popular in far northern areas where ice often becomes so thick anglers can drive their cars onto the lakes.

A far less expensive alternative, which I rely upon when the ice is less than eight inches thick, is a spud bar you can make yourself. Mine consists of several 12-inch pieces of threaded pipe and assorted collars that allow the spud to be assembled on location. Sticking out of one of the pipe section ends is a wide-faced chisel I had a local shop weld in place for a dollar.

In addition to a means of cutting holes in the ice, you'll need an assortment of tip-ups, fishing rods, minnow bucket, assorted live baits and artificial lures, perhaps a thermos bottle of coffee or hot soup, a small camp stool to sit on, and other gear. We'll discuss all of these in a moment, but meanwhile it's necessary to acquire some means of transporting all this paraphernalia across the frozen surface of the lake.

The easiest tack is to borrow a child's sled, mount an orange crate on top, and simply pull it behind you as you walk. I've also seen some anglers don backpacks and in each hand carry a plastic five-gallon pail filled with still other gear.

Being hopelessly addicted to the sport, I built an ice-fishing truck and over the years have seen similar designs concocted by others. My particular creation features wide-flotation runners, a padded seat, and a storage compartment which holds not only all my fishing tackle and bait but other gear such as a camera, spare gloves, disassembled spud bar and such. There is even a semi-open front for housing a catalytic heater or gasoline lantern. Both put out a tremendous amount of heat, and the lantern aids in night-fishing, when you can have some of the hottest action.

THE SHOW BEGINS WITH TIP-UPS

Most ice fishermen use two types of tackle: a combination of tip-ups and lightweight rods that enable them to have numerous lines in the water simultaneously and thereby greatly increase their chances of catching not only plenty of fish but a variety of different species.

Tip-ups generally cost less than $6 apiece and since they are baited with worms or small minnows they are used exclusively for larger panfish such as yellow perch, slab crappies, rock bass, white bass, and jumbo sunfish.

Although tip-up designs may differ slightly, all operate in basically the same manner. A simple reel is affixed to a shaft that is submerged in the water just beneath the surface of the ice. You don't need to worry about the reel being underwater because most tip-up reels are constructed of cheap metal or plastic, with a minimum of moving parts. Cross-members made of wood or plastic hold the affair in place from above. When a fish takes the bait, the reel automatically pays out line so the fish feels no resistance. Meanwhile, a brightly colored flag simultaneously pops up to signal the strike. Then the angler rushes to the scene, gently sets the hook, then brings his fish in by pulling the line hand over hand.

I usually like to place my tip-ups in a straight line, spaced about twenty yards apart, and running from relatively shallow water out to deeper

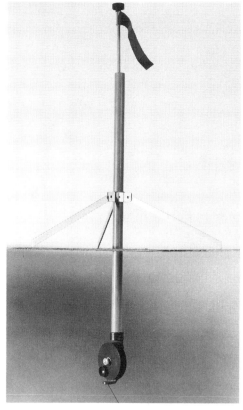

Tip-ups come in many designs and are intended for fishing with live baits. When a fish takes a bait, a flag pops up to signal the strike. This tip-up has a spring-loaded flag rather than a wire arm. Reel is always submerged beneath ice.

water. The straight-line placement of the tip-ups allows me to glance down the line and see any flag which has been triggered. And by simultaneously test-fishing many different depth levels, I'm able to locate fish in that particular area. If one specific tip-up begins to produce fish consistently while the others are not, I cut a series of new holes at the same depth level as the productive tip-up, with the straight line now running perpendicular to the first series of holes which were cut.

Live minnows are undeniably the best baits to use with tip-ups, but sometimes they are difficult to find during the winter. In this case, dead minnows are next best. These can be minnows put up in a preservative solution in glass bottles or freeze-dried minnows in plastic bags that "reconstitute" into soft food once in the water. If you have excess minnows left over from summer fishing outings, place them in plastic bags in your freezer and save them for ice

fishing adventures later in the year. In addition to minnows, I like to bait at least a couple of tip-ups with small garden worms. Upon occasion, for reasons only the fish can explain, worms will far out-fish minnows.

Winter fish are less aggressive feeders, and light lines are therefore the rule. I usually like to spool about forty yards of 4-pound monofilament on the reels affixed to my tip-ups. But if I'm in the vicinity of thick weedbeds early in the ice fishing season, or in tangled brush and timber in later weeks, I occasionally switch to 6-pound line. To the terminal end of the line, tie a size 10, long-shanked hook and just above it pinch a split-shot to take the bait down.

Generally, I like to lower the bait all the way down until slack line tells me it is on the bottom. Then I turn the reel handle one revolution to suspend the bait about a foot above the lake floor. Next, I place the flag in its cocked position, and sit down and play the waiting game.

With numerous tip-ups in place, ice anglers also use short rods to fish live baits or lures. Many anglers make their own rods from discarded or broken tip sections from spinning or fly rods.

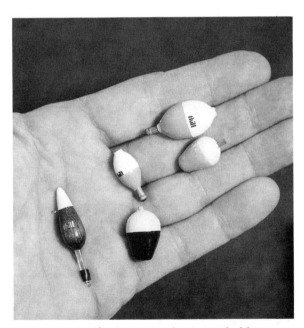

When fishing live baits, use the tiniest bobbers you can find because bites are barely perceptible. These are Thill floats.

JIGGING FOR PANFISH

Actually, "playing the waiting game" is a misnomer because few ice fishermen merely stand around with their hands in their pockets waiting for tip-up flags to pop into view. A majority of anglers meanwhile cut still another hole or two in the ice and begin using light ice fishing rods or *jigglesticks* to fish live baits or artificial lures for panfish.

Some anglers purchase factory-made jigging rods, which consist of an 18-inch wooden handle and an 18-inch length of fiberglass rod with just one or two guides. The reel will invariably be nothing more than two opposing pegs around which the line is hand-wound. I recommend 2-pound test, or 4-pound at the most.

Many other anglers prefer to make their own rods, using the discarded tip sections from old or broken spinning or fly rods, cut off to 18 inches in length, with the butt section inserted into a length of wooden dowel. Then they tape a small fly reel or spinning reel to the handle.

I traditionally begin using my jigging rod to fish live baits by tying a size 10 long-shanked gold hook to the terminal end of the line, adding a split-shot for weight, lowering the rig to the bottom to determine the depth, and then placing a tiny bobber on the line so the bait will be about a foot off the bottom. The bobber can be made of plastic, foam, or cork, but it should

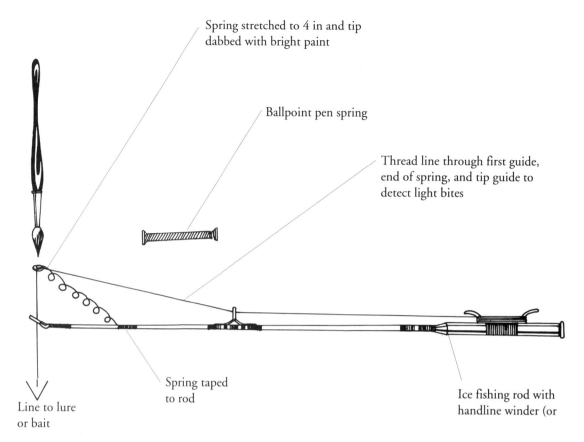

Spring stretched to 4 in and tip dabbed with bright paint

Ballpoint pen spring

Thread line through first guide, end of spring, and tip guide to detect light bites

Spring taped to rod

Line to lure or bait

Ice fishing rod with handline winder (or

A homemade spring-bobber attached to the rod tip allows an angler to feel even the lightest bites.

be very tiny, no larger than a dime.

If the fish are biting very lightly, however, many anglers dispense with a bobber and simply curl their index finger around the line to detect the subtle "ticks" that indicate strikes.

Still other anglers attach a spring-bobber to their rod tips. A spring-bobber is a very fine piece of wire, sporting a brightly colored bead at its end, that serves as an extension to the rod tip and will visually telegraph strikes you may not even be able to feel with your bare hands. Spring-bobbers can be purchased in tackleshops, but you can make your own by simply using the spring from a discarded ballpoint pen. Stretch the spring to about 4 inches in length, tape one end to your rod tip, then run your line through the center. A dab

of fluorescent paint at the end takes the place of the bead.

For bait, the best choices are mealworms, mousies, waxworms, or any of several other larval forms that may be available at local baitshops. You can also buy a tin of freeze-dried "maggies," which reconstitute into soft food when water is added to the can.

It may be necessary to punch holes through the ice in several different locations (in the immediate vicinity of your tip-ups) and test-fish the water before fish are located. Yet once a good panfish population has been pinpointed and the action has started, you can sometimes pull in fish as fast as you can lower a baited hook to the bottom. This is when I dispense with the time-consuming process of rebaiting

Best artificial lures for smaller panfish species such as bluegills and sunfish are tiny jigs and ice flies. Note simple line winding device on rod handle.

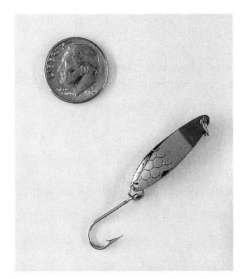

For larger panfish such as crappies and perch, small ice fishing spoons produce better results than jigs or ice flies.

When fishing jigs, ice flies, or ice spoons, raise the rod tip to the vertical position, then slowly lower it to the surface of the ice. Most strikes will come as the lure is sinking with a fluttering motion.

Different panfish bite best under different conditions. Bluegills and sunfish are caught in greatest numbers very early in winter, while yellow perch fishing is better later in the season.

hooks and reach for a second, pre-rigged ice fishing rod that has an artificial lure tied on.

These lures are generically referred to as "ice flies," but they are not flies in the traditional sense. Rather, they are tiny, teardrop-shaped metal jigs and spoonlike affairs in very bright colors—silver, gold, red, yellow, chartreuse, or orange. Often, a tiny bit of feather or fur adorns the hook. On a given day, be sure to experiment with a variety of colors because the fish often exhibit definite preferences.

The technique of jigging with ice flies is quite easy even for first-timers to master. Begin by lowering the jig all the way to the bottom. Then, in slow motion, raise your rod tip two or three feet. Next, begin slowly lowering your rod tip so the jig will begin sinking. Most strikes come as the jig is settling downward and rock-ing back and forth with a slight fluttering or quivering motion, so be prepared to set the hook lightly when you feel even a slight "bump."

TRICKS OF THE TRADE

During winter, there are a number of behavior nuances of certain panfish species that are worth mentioning here.

Ice fishing for *yellow perch* is unquestionably best toward the end of the winter season because, once open water arrives, the species is among the first to spawn. Consequently, as early as January they may already be on the move toward shallower water in preparation for their mating rituals, and this makes them much

If snow cover is patchy, cut your holes where there is snow rather than where there is snow-free ice. Note ladle for skimming ice chips from the hole.

easier to catch than during midwinter when they may still be in very deep water. Look for them on the steep points that guard the entrances to large bays and coves, or in the bays themselves, at depths of less than ten feet. Unlike other panfishes which are found near weed growth early in the season and then later make a transition to woody or rocky cover, perch prefer clean sandy bottoms throughout the entire ice fishing season. The best time to catch them seems to be midday.

Conversely, *bluegills* and *sunfish* are active very early in the season, as soon as the ice is safe to walk on. Begin searching for them in weedy areas as discussed earlier. Yet keep in mind that bluegills and sunfish require higher levels of dissolved oxygen in the water than other panfishes. Consequently, as the season wears on, these species are the first to leave vegetative areas which are beginning to decompose in order to relocate themselves in woody cover or rocky bottom habitat. Bluegills and sunfish are eager biters all day long and continuing through the night hours. If you see distant lantern lights winking in the darkness, the anglers are after bluegills and sunfish and you're welcome to join the fun!

Crappies frequently find themselves mixed in with bluegills and sunfish but only when they are holding in deeper water than usual. If you're catching only bluegills and sunfish in a given area, that tells you there may also be crappies there. Move still farther away from the shoreline, where the water is at least ten feet deeper, and you'll probably catch crappies exclusively. Crappies are more adverse to bright light than most other panfish, so if there is no blanket of snow covering the ice, restrict your fishing to cloudy days for the best success.

White bass continue to exhibit their schooling tendencies and nomadic travels throughout the winter, which means catching them is a hit or miss proposition. You'll likely be fishing for something else, suddenly see a flurry of white bass action, but then not catch another white bass the rest of the winter.

Rock bass, yellow bass, white perch, and *chain pickerel* constitute incidental bonus catches during the winter. They are not heavy winter feeders and, therefore, anglers seldom target them specifically.

Finally, here is a pot pourri of tackle and helpful hints.

Many anglers chum for panfish beneath the ice by cutting one particular chum hole within the midst of their tip-ups and jigging rod endeavors. Into that hole, they lower a can of sardines (packed in oil) on a length of string after first punching holes in the can. The oil and fish odor that exudes is believed to attract all species of panfish.

After cutting a hole in the ice, it will be filled with ice chips. Include an old soup ladle in your gear to clear the hole and also remove skim ice that eventually begins to form.

The best ice fishing conditions invariably see a blanket of snow over the entire lake to reduce light penetration from the sun.

If there is no snow cover, fish earlier and later than usual when the sun is low on the horizon. If the lake is only partially snow-covered, cut your fishing holes where there are patches of snow rather than in clean, snow-free areas.

If the sun is bright, and you're not catching fish on or near the bottom, raise your lures or bait in several foot increments to test-fish levels closer to the ice. In bright sunlight, zooplankton rises upward toward the light source, baitfish follow, and panfish follow the forage.

Sunglasses are vital to protect your eyes from the bright glare of the snow and ice. And a pair of "creepers," or inexpensive cleats, made for the purpose and strapped to your boots will prevent you from slipping and sliding.

At the outset of each day, as a safety measure, cut a hole in the ice close to shore to check its thickness before venturing out onto the lake to fish. The ice should be a minimum of three inches thick.

15

Cooking the Catch

Many sports offer the rewards of fresh air, exercise, relaxation, and a needed break from everyday routine.

Yet fishing is unique because the angler enjoys the added benefit of bringing home fresh, delicious food that will please even the most discriminating tastebuds of friends and family. Additionally, fresh fish is low in fat and cholesterol, high in protein, high in vitamins and minerals, and therefore one of the most nutritious foods to make a part of anyone's regular diet.

One thing is crucial in the preparation of panfish for the table: No matter which species you've caught, or which recipe you may follow, the quality of the finished dish depends primarily on how the fish was handled to begin with. For this reason, properly caring for one's catch becomes of paramount concern the very moment the fish is landed.

ONBOARD FISH STORAGE

At last count I owned about five fish stringers, some made of cord and others of the chain vari-

ety with wire snaps, but I'll confess that I rarely use any of them during a day of panfishing. They are simply tucked away somewhere and brought out for brief minutes at the end of the day when I want to secure several fish on the snaps in order to take a picture.

Most often, when working from small craft, I rely instead upon a wire fish basket that clamps onto the boat's gunnel, or a nylon mesh bag of similar design, both of which have wide mouths that allow a fish to be quickly inserted. These gizmos do a far better job than a stringer in keeping fish alive for long hours, plus they afford the utmost convenience when the action is fast and furious and fish are coming aboard on almost every cast. On a larger boat having an aerated live well, the task is equally easy.

Yet I dispense even with these fish storage methods when the season progresses to the point that the water temperature begins exceeding 60 degrees. Now, retaining the utmost fish flavor and freshness is best accomplished with a camp cooler on board.

Regardless of the cooler's design or size, maxi-

In addition to enjoyable recreation, panfishermen bring home food for the table that is tasty and highly nutritious.

mum cooling efficiency is gained by using shaved or crushed ice, or cubes, rather than block ice. On top of the ice place several plastic bags. I prefer the zip-loc poly type in one-gallon sizes. Each bag will hold an average of six to eight panfish.

Each time you boat a fish you want to keep for the table, immediately give it a sharp rap over the head just behind the eyes to kill it. Then place it in the plastic bag, close the opening and completely bury it in the ice. With this technique there is no muss, no fuss, no risk of loose fish soaking in meltwater that may begin to accumulate in the bottom of the cooler, and there is no messy ice chest to clean later. But most important of all, no matter

what the temperature that day, your fish will remain icy cold and in perfect condition.

SHORESIDE FISH STORAGE

A vast number of panfishermen do not use boats on every outing, preferring instead to hike along the shorelines of ponds or small lakes or don hip boots to wade shallow rivers and streams.

In these instances, some type of stringer, secured to a shoreline root or the belt of one's waders, will undoubtedly prove the most efficient, yet there are right and wrong ways to use

Securing fish on a stringer makes a nice photo at day's end, but during the day other storage methods do a better job of preserving all the flavor you've caught.

A wire fish basket that clamps to the boat's gunnel keeps fish frisky and permits them to be retained quickly when the action is fast and furious.

In warm weather, best bet is an iced-down camping cooler onboard to quickly chill the fish and prevent spoilage.

them. When securing fish on a stringer, don't run the cord or metal snap through the fish's gill-cover opening and out the mouth, as this will kill it in short order. Simply run the stringer once through the lower jaw and the fish will be sufficiently secured.

An alternative to using a stringer that many anglers favor is a wicker or canvas creel that hangs from the shoulder like a large purse. When using such a creel it is not necessary to place fish in plastic bags as no ice is involved, and hence, there is no accumulation of meltwater. I partially fill the creel with fresh green ferns or aquatic weeds that first have been soaked with water and then only slightly wrung out. I place the fish in the creel on top of a layer of the vegetation, then cover the catch with additional damp ferns or weeds.

However, once midsummer arrives, more stringent measures should be taken to preserve fish. A stringer still can be used, or a creel, but once several fish have been accumulated, or a half-hour has passed, transfer the fish to a colder environment. In some cases, if you've been able to park your vehicle not far from the water's edge, an ice-filled cooler is the easiest solution. Otherwise, if a bit of hiking is involved, an insulated picnic bag works very well. Buy a bag of the size designed to hold a pair of two-quart thermos bottles and you'll have plenty of room for not only your fish but a sandwich and cold drink. Then, simply set it in the shade of a nearby tree while fishing and periodically relocate it as you work your way down the shoreline.

Using ice with one of these picnic bags is somewhat difficult and often messy. I prefer one of those thin, rectangular, reusable ice packs you can buy in any camping supply store. These gizmos are filled with liquid refrigerant, completely sealed, and intended to be placed in your home freezer until they are frozen solid. You can then transfer such an ice pack to your picnic bag and it will efficiently chill everything inside for about twelve hours.

When wading a river, or fishing a small lake from the bank, a wicker or canvas creel filled with damp ferns is an excellent way to care for your catch.

Meanwhile, fish stored in your picnic bag should first be inserted into a large Ziploc poly bag to eliminate messy clean-up.

HOW TO FILLET AND ROUGH-DRESS PANFISH

Some anglers who are about to clean a large number of fish like to don a pair of lightweight cotton gloves. Even when wet, such gloves ensure a firm grasp and also eliminate the otherwise inevitable feeling of "sandpaper hands" when the job is done.

All panfish can be filleted but there are two distinctly different ways, depending upon the species in question. The elongated panfishes, such as perch, white bass, pickerel, and larger crappies, can be filleted just the same as you would a bass or walleye. Simply follow the step-by-step photos presented here.

The smaller panfishes, or those of high-body profile, such as bluegills, sunfish, and rock bass, should be filleted in a different manner, also shown here. With this technique, you'll acquire two fillets each about the size of a jumbo shrimp, which can be cooked in a variety of ways we'll describe later.

Both of these methods are quick and easy because there is no need to cut off the head of the fish, no need to remove the gills or innards or anything else. Rather, we merely remove the fillet slabs themselves from the sides of the fish, then throw the remaining carcass, still in one piece, into the trash can.

One slight variation to both methods, which some anglers prefer, is to omit the last step and leave the skin on the fillets. This may be especially desirable with such species as yellow perch, white bass, yellow bass, and crappies because when the fish is fried the skin crisps nicely and turns a delicious golden brown; moreover, if the fillet slabs are large enough to be broiled, the skin prevents the fillets from sticking to the grill. However, it is necessary, before following the actual filleting sequence, to remove the fish's scales with a small scaling tool made for the purpose, or a dull knife blade, moving against the lay of the

HOW TO FILLET A PANFISH (1)

1. To fillet elongated panfish such as perch, begin by making an angular cut as shown, but stop the blade as soon as it contacts bone.

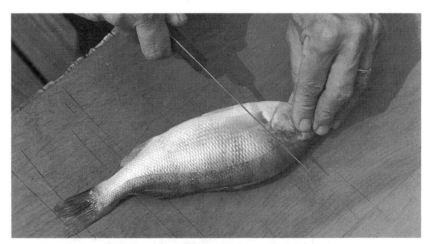

2. Turn the blade sideways and run it the length of the body, keeping it close to the backbone. Do not cut the fillet free when you reach the tail.

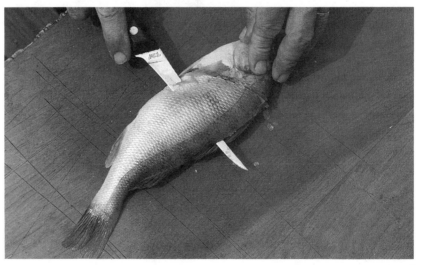

continued

3. Then turn the fish with the meat up and slide the blade between the skin and fillet to remove the skin.

4. Two delicious, boneless fillets in only thirty seconds, with the remaining carcass left intact.

HOW TO FILLET A PANFISH (2)

1. To fillet a fish with a high body profile, such as a bluegill, begin by making the same angular cut.

continued

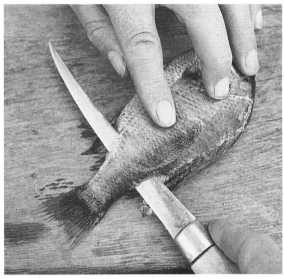

2. Insert just the tip of your knife until it stops against the ribcage and follow the backbone all the way to the rear of the dorsal fin.

3. Then push the tip of the knife all the way through the flesh and slice the remainder of the way to the tail.

4. With the tip of the blade, follow the curvature of the ribcage and the entire fillet should pop out of its pocket.

5. Finally, remove the skin in the same manner as before.

continued

6. Two perfect fillets, each about the size of a jumbo shrimp, with the carcass. Although this method looks complicated, the author can fillet three bluegills per minute!

HOW TO ROUGH-DRESS PANFISH

1. To rough-dress panfish, begin by removing the scales by briskly rubbing the blade against the grain.

2. Prop the fish on edge and cut the head and gills free. Note the curvature of the cut, which preserves the upper shoulder meat.

continued

3. Make this cut as shown, all the way through, to remove the vent area, and finish by scooping out the entrails with the tip of your finger.

4. Whole rough-dressed fish should look like this. Note that the tail was not removed. When fried crisp, it is delicious. The dorsal fin is easily removed at the table by grabbing it at the rear and pulling forward.

scales with short, brisk strokes of the hand.

In some instances, rough-dressed fish may be more desirable than those which have been filleted. Rough-dressing means first removing the scales, then cleaning the fish in such a manner that the head and innards are removed but the meat is otherwise left on the skeleton. Step-by-step photos in this section show you how.

HOW TO FREEZE AND DEFROST PANFISH

Properly transporting your fish home and cleaning them is only the first step in ensuring toothsome delights for the dinner table. Now, you must store the fish properly.

If part of the catch is to be eaten within three days, wrap the fillets or rough-dressed fish in several paper towels that have been soaked with water and wrung out, next place the works in a gallon-size zip-lock poly bag and then set the package in your refrigerator. The damp toweling within the enclosed bag will keep the fish moist.

If the fish are to be saved for later use, you'll have to freeze them. In a frozen state, all species of panfish will remain in excellent condition for up to nine months. Nevertheless, there are a few important tips to keep in mind.

We've found that the best way to freeze fish is in plastic freezer bags intended for garden vegetables. We usually use the one-quart size.

After the fish have been placed in the bag, bunch up the neck between your thumb and forefinger, raise the mouth to your lips, and inhale deeply to suck all the air out of the bag. This will cause the walls of the bag to collapse tightly around the fish, ensuring a complete seal with no air left to cause rancidity or freezer burn. As soon as the bag collapses, pinch the neck tightly, twist it several times, then secure with a wire twist-tie.

Of course, always remember to label the outside of each package of fish with the name of the species, the approximate quantity, and the date the fish went into the freezer.

To defrost fish, don't make the mistake of simply setting a frozen package on the drainboard in your sink because the outside will defrost first and that portion of the fish will begin to reach room temperature and dry out while the inside areas still remain frozen for many hours.

Instead, anticipate your dining plans and transfer your plastic bags of frozen fish from the freezer to your refrigerator the night before you plan to cook the fish. In this manner, the fish will defrost slowly and remain icy cold all the while.

BASIC FRYING TECHNIQUES

Fish flavors can vary enormously between species. But all fish are unique in the sense that unlike red meat, fish flesh possesses little or no connective tissue and therefore always cooks quickly and if not overdone (a cardinal sin) is always tender, even though the flesh of certain species is of a coarser grain and to the palate seems more dense in texture.

Unquestionably, the most popular method of preparing the panfish species is by frying them, simply because few of the fish an angler catches will be sufficiently thick to warrant conventional baking or broiling methods. In fact, if you tried to bake bluegill fillets, for example, you'd undoubtedly accomplish little more than drying them out. There are exceptions, however, as we'll discuss later, in which certain panfish can indeed be broiled and cooked by still other means.

Whatever the species to be fried, I suggest the use of a heavy, cast-iron skillet or a pan coated with Teflon or Silverstone. Frypans entirely of steel or aluminum do not evenly disperse the heat over the metal's cooking surface; as a result, hot spots often develop here and there, sometimes scorching parts of the fish.

We prefer to use about 1/8-inch of vegetable oil such as Mazola and the ideal temperature for frying fish is 370 degrees. When using a conventional kitchen stove, a cooking thermometer that clips onto the frying pan is handy for maintaining this temperature. Some of the countertop deep-fryers on the market that utilize wire baskets, as well as those fueled by propane and are intended for outside use, have

When frying fish, temperature control is critical. With a conventional stove, use a cooking thermometer. With deep-fryers like this one, install a temperature gauge.

a temperature dial to regulate the heat. If you are using a gasoline campstove, and don't have a cooking thermometer, you can "guesstimate" the proper temperature by simply dropping a small cube of bread into the hot oil; when it begins to bubble, dance around and turn brown around the edges, the oil is ready.

When frying fish, I always try to keep the fillets or whole fish very cold before they are slipped into the cooking oil. The reaction between the hot oil and cold fish puts a sealing crust on the fish which prevents the inner flesh from absorbing oil and becoming soggy and greasy tasting.

Also make sure that you place only a few pieces of fish into the skillet at a time and then wait at least a full minute before adding a few more pieces. Otherwise, overloading the skillet or wire basket all at once with cold fish will drastically lower the temperature of the cooking oil, requiring a much longer cooking time, and results in the fish becoming dried out rather than remaining moist and flaky.

When the first fish placed in the oil becomes brown and crisp around the edges, and light golden everywhere else, they are done. Carefully transfer them from the skillet or wire basket to a platter covered with a thick layer of paper towels so the fish will drain, and then place the platter in an oven preheated to 200 degrees so the fish will remain hot. If no oven is available, at least tightly cover the platter with aluminum foil. Then add still more fillets or rough-dressed fish to the oil and prepare to remove the other fish which should now be approaching doneness.

If it sounds like I'm neurotically fussy about

these various steps in frying fish, you're right! Nine times in ten it is not the particular batter, mix, or other ingredients that determine the end result, but the care with which each of the various steps is followed.

There is such a plethora of fish recipes that entire books have been written on the subject! But since this is not a cookbook, I'll include here only those special few that my dinner guests repeatedly ask for over and again.

The two most widely accepted frying recipes are the dry dusting method and the wet dunking method. When dry dusting, the fillets or whole dressed fish are dipped in a liquid solution and then rolled in a dry medium such as flour before being added to the pan. The wet

When using a campstove, a failsafe way of knowing your cooking oil is ready for the fish is to drop a cube of bread into the oil. If it sputters and begins turning brown, the oil is ready.

dunking method involves the creation of a batter-like mix: the fish are briefly dipped in the batter bowl, extracted, excess batter is allowed to drip off, and then the fish are submitted to the pan or wire basket.

Basic Dry Dusting Recipe

    1 cup flour
    1 can evaporated milk
    1 tsp. each salt & pepper
    cooking oil

Blend together the salt, pepper, and flour. With paper toweling, pat dry the panfish fillets or whole, rough-dressed fish. Dip the individual fillets or dressed fish in the milk, dredge in the seasoned flour, then slide into the hot oil.

Basic Wet Dunking Mix

    1 cup flour
    2 eggs
    1 tsp. baking powder
    ½ cup water
    1 tsp. sugar
    cooking oil

Blend all ingredients in a bowl, adding just a bit more water if the created batter is not runny enough to drip from a spoon. With paper toweling, pat dry the fish fillets or whole, rough-dressed fish. Next, dunk the individual fillets or fish into the mix, allow excess batter to drip away, then add the fish to the oil.

The two basic methods described above are perfect for all panfish species. The only difference between using white bass, for example, or bluegills, is that you'll achieve a slight variation in a nevertheless delightful flavor.

Moreover, I encourage the reader to experiment on his own. For example, with either method above, try substituting cornmeal for white flour. Or, use whole wheat flour, finely ground bread crumbs, finely crushed potato chips, finely crushed crackers (saltines, cheese crackers, rye crackers, etc.) or whatever you have on hand.

By the same token, instead of using the evaporated milk in the dry dusting method, or the water in the wet dunking method, try substituting buttermilk, 7-Up, ginger ale, or even beer! All are excellent and result in an entirely different flavor. Chances are you may even discover a new taste treat you like even better than the substitutions recommended here.

It's also possible to achieve an endless number of still other variations through the addition of spices or seasonings. For example, instead of salt and pepper, use an equal quantity of Lawry's Seasoned Salt, or a touch of garlic powder, or perhaps lemon pepper, onion salt, celery salt, chili powder, or just a touch of red cayenne pepper or oregano.

Instead of conventional corn oil, try peanut oil. Or, add several healthy shots of tabasco sauce to the oil. Or, add several tablespoons of bacon drippings to the oil.

With these basic ideas at hand, you can achieve so many different combinations of recipes it will take you years to try them all.

BROILING PANFISH

Broiling meat probably dates back almost as far as the first uses of fire. Today, the principles of broiling are the same; in most cases, we simply use more modern equipment.

However, when it comes to panfish, there are certain rules of thumb I suggest following. First, it always is better to use fillets rather than whole, rough-dressed fish. Second, the larger the fillet slabs the better. This means you'll undoubtedly have your best success with the elongated species such as yellow perch, chain pickerel, white bass, and in some cases yellow bass and white perch.

When using the broiler in your oven at home, the fish should be placed approximately three or four inches from the heat source and as they cook they should be turned only once.

But when broiling fish outdoors, the technique differs slightly. First, it's better to broil over coals than over open flames. Charcoal can be used, but better are hardwood chunks which have burned down to white embers. Moreover, I recommend using a special fish broiling device made for the purpose. One popular brand is Griffo, which consists of a perforated metal grid to prevent the fish from falling through the larger spaces found on a conventional grill.

Begin by placing the fish (on the broiling rack) about two inches from the heat source for just one minute to seal in the juices, turn the fish once and broil on the opposite side for another minute. Then, raise the broiling rack to six inches above the heat source to finish the cooking.

Whether broiling outdoors or indoors, baste the fish to impart flavor, achieve a bronzed finish, and prevent it from drying out. The best basting mixture I've come upon is equal portions of melted butter and olive oil, with just a touch of lemon juice. Toward the end of the broiling you may also wish to sprinkle a bit of paprika on the fillets, but feel free to experiment by trying onion salt, celery salt, or one of the Celestial Seasonings products. But, above all, prick the fillets a bit as they broil to ensure that they are not permitted to overcook. When the meat flakes easily, the fish are done and should immediately be removed from the heat source.

STEWS AND CHOWDERS

As the season draws to a close, anglers frequently begin cleaning out their freezers, making room for small game, upland birds, waterfowl, and hopefully, venison. The question is what to do with any remnants of remaining fish? Perhaps there is one package with a few white bass fillets, a smallish container of bluegills, a lone chain pickerel, but not really enough fish to make an entire meal of just one species.

Why not make a chowder? A chowder is ideally suited to miscellaneous fish species cooked together, it takes almost no time at all, and you can be creative by throwing into the pot any random vegetables at hand. Moreover, if there is any leftover chowder, which is not likely, it freezes very well and is a welcome meal on short notice during some cold winter night. It's not even necessary to defrost it; simply remove the frozen chowder from its freezer container, place in a pot and on very low heat bring it to a gentle simmer.

My favorite chowder begins by frying in a skillet until crisp strips of bacon cut into small pieces. When the bacon is done, remove it from the pan and set it aside on a paper towel to drain. Now, in the same bacon fat, sauté two large onions which have been chopped. Transfer the fat and onion to a large pot, add a pound or two of random fish species which have been cut up into bite-size pieces. If some of the fish you've defrosted are in whole, rough-dressed form, fillet the meat away from the bones.

Next, add to the pot four diced potatoes, one teaspoon salt, one teaspoon pepper, one teaspoon blended herbs (your choice), and three cups of water. Let this simmer, covered, on low heat until the potatoes and fish are tender (about an hour). Then stir in one can of condensed "cream" soup, such as cream of mushroom or cream of celery, and then a half cup of canned milk. Let the works simmer for another half-hour, being sure it does not come to a boil.

Serve the chowder in deep bowls, with the bacon bits sprinkled on top, and with plenty of crackers.

To vary the chowder routine, some cooks add a diced green pepper, or almost any other vegetable at hand such as diced carrots, celery, turnips, or kohlrabi.

BOILED FISH

It doesn't have a very fancy name, but boiled fish is an elegant way to prepare any of the panfishes.

In a skillet, place four potatoes which have been peeled and quartered, one onion sliced thin, one bay leaf, two whole cloves, ½ teaspoon salt and ¼ teaspoon pepper. Barely cover all of this with cold water, place a lid on the skillet, and simmer over low heat until the potatoes are one-half done.

Next, lay any species of panfish fillets (yellow perch, white perch, white bass, yellow bass, or crappies are recommended) on top of the potatoes and other ingredients, cover, and continue simmering until both the fish and potatoes are done.

Next, remove the fish to a plate and put them someplace to keep them warm. Scald a quarter-cup of evaporated milk and then blend in 1 teaspoon of flour. Stir this into the potatoes and other ingredients and let it bubble a bit until a rich gravy has formed and then pour the sauce over the fish and serve. This meal, while taking a bit longer than other recipes, will draw rave reviews from your guests.

Not many anglers are aware of it, but panfish are also very good served cold. Here are two ideas I am sure you will like.

Heat a kettle of salted water to boiling and add a packet of shrimp or crab boiling seasoning. Drop into the water fish fillets or whole, rough-dressed fish. Cover the pot and let the fish cook for about two minutes, no longer! Remove the fish from the water, separate the meat from the bones if necessary, wrap the fish in foil and then place in your refrigerator overnight. The following day, shred the meat with a fork and mix into a robust chef's salad. Served this way, it is difficult to tell the difference between panfish and crab or lobster.

Finally, my friend Bill Gressard of Ravenna, Ohio, makes a panfish cocktail which goes well with any meal. It's also superb as an *hors d'oeuvre* when your crew is anxiously waiting for you to finish cooking the main course.

Fillet several dozen panfish (bluegills or sunfish are the preferred species, but any others can be used as well). From each fish you'll get two pieces of meat, each about the size of a jumbo shrimp.

Place the fillets in a steamer. Cover and let the fish steam for one minute, no more. Next, remove the fish, place them on a plate and transfer to your freezer for ten minutes to chill. Serve with any kind of seafood sauce, as you would shrimp cocktail.

16

Panfishing Across North America

United States

An entire book could be devoted to the tens of thousands of panfishing waters in the United States. As a result, the following state listings are by no means complete but merely reflect some of the more popular locations for catching various species.

Use this section as a valuable reference in planning panfishing outings. In this manner, an angler intending to visit Kentucky, for example, can thumb to the Kentucky section and immediately determine which panfish species are most plentiful in the state and which particular waters are worth consideration during upcoming fishing outings. At that point, all that remains is for him to write to the state fish and game department (addresses given) to obtain a copy of the current fishing regulations and whatever maps he needs showing lakeside facilities.

ALABAMA

Not even the state's resident fishery biologists are certain how many square miles of panfishing water exist in Alabama for there are literally

thousands of unnamed ponds, sloughs and backwaters teeming with fish.

This is, of course, in addition to a number of the largest lakes and reservoirs to be found anywhere in the country. Following are recommended lakes for various species. For more information contact the Department of Conservation & Natural Resources, Division of Game & Fish, 64 N. Union St., Montgomery, AL 36130.

Bluegills: Ketona, Guntersville, Tuscaloosa, Yates, Thurlow, Jackson, Claiborne, Miller's Ferry, Shelby, Aliceville, Bankhead, R.L. Harris.

Crappies: Lay, Aliceville, Weiss, Bankhead, Wheeler, Neely Henry, Guntersville, Pickwick, Lewis-Smith, Holt, Jones, Warrior, Yates, Martin, Grant, Eufaula, Millers Ferry.

White Bass: Wheeler, Pickwick, Lewis-Smith, Weiss, Wilson, Logan, Grant, Warrior River.

Yellow Bass: Inland.

Sunfishes (redbreast, redear, green, longear): Chattahoochee, Wilson, Gannt, Point A, Shelby, Bayview, Opelika.

Chain Pickerel: Dyas, Warrior, Millers Ferry, Eufaula.

Yellow Perch: Harding, Guntersville.

ARIZONA

Primarily desert, Arizona nevertheless offers a surprising number of panfishing opportunities, most of which are in large impoundments formed by the damming of major river systems.

For more information, contact the Game & Fish Department, 2221 West Greenway Rd., Phoenix, AZ 85023.

Bluegills: San Carlos, Canyon, Imperial-Laguna, Alamo.

Crappies: Pleasant, San Carlos, Lake Mead, Mohave, Havasu, Lyman, Powell, Canyon, Topock Marsh, Apache, Bartlett, Horseshoe, Roosevelt, Saguaro, Parker Canyon, Verde River.

White Bass: Imperial.

Sunfishes (green, redear, warmouth): Col-

Despite its desert appearance, Arizona offers numerous panfishing opportunities, mostly in large impoundments.

orado River, Cholla, Havasu, Mead, Mohave, Powell, Topock Marsh, Apache, Bartlett, Canyon, Horseshoe, Pleasant, Roosevelt, Saguaro, Verde River, Parker Canyon, Alamo.

Yellow Bass: Saguaro, Canyon, Imperial-Laguna, Apache, Canyon, Horseshoe, Roosevelt, Verde River.

ARKANSAS

Arkansas, situated in the beautiful Ozark Mountains, is one of our premier panfishing states. With over 9,000 miles of rivers and streams, 600,000 acres of lakes and reservoirs, and countless bayous and sloughs, an angler could devote a lifetime to fishing "The Natural State" and not even scratch the surface of available panfishing opportunities.

For more information, contact the Game & Fish Commission, No. 2 Natural Resources Dr., Little Rock, AR 72205.

Bluegills: Blue Mountain, Dardanelle, Greeson, Millwood, Ouachita, Ozark, Van Buren City, Grampus, Wallace, White Oak, Wilhelmena, Wilson, Belco, Beulah, Big Hurricane, Big Lake, Felsenthal, Grand.

Crappies: Roosevelt, Beaver, Blue Mountain, Dardanelle, Greers Ferry, Greeson, Millwood, Nimrod, Ouachita, Ozark, Table Rock, Beaver Fork, Grampus,

White Bass: Arkansas River, Beaver, Bull Shoals, Norfork, Greers Ferry, Ouachita, Millwood, Roosevelt, Dardanelle, DeGray, Millwood, Ozark, Table Rock.

Redear Sunfish: Bear Creek, Millwood, Beaver Fork, Booneville, Sugar Loaf, Tri-County, Truman Baker, White Oak, Welhelmena, First Old River.

Longear Sunfish: Mirror, Greeson, Tri-County, Big Lake.

Green Sunfish: Blue Mountain, Nimrod, Carol Cross, Horsehead, Van Buren City, Lou Emma, Truman Baker.

Warmouth: Booneville, Greenwood, Hamilton, Ozark, Barnett, Big Hurricane, Horsede, Shirey Bay, White River, Spring River.

Chain Pickerel: Ouachita, Ft Chaffee, Iron Forks, Conway, Cox Creek, Enterprise, Grampus, Greenlee, Overcup, Little Red River.

Yellow Bass: Calion, Big Lake.

Rock Bass: Norfork.

CALIFORNIA

Long on sunshine and short on winter-like weather, California offers numerous fishing opportunities.

Unfortunately, the focus has been on its largemouth bass, trout and salmon, and saltwater fisheries, and the state does not maintain listings of waters inhabited by specific panfish species.

The exception pertains to state records taken from the following waters:

Bluegill: Lake Los Serranos.

Black Crappie: Mendota Pool.

White Crappie: Clear Lake.

White Bass: Ferguson Lake.

Redear Sunfish: Lake Casitas.

For more information, contact the Department of Fish & Game, Fisheries Division, 1416

Ninth St., Sacramento, CA 95814.

COLORADO

Primarily a mountainous trout state, Colorado nevertheless is a land of contrast. Much of the eastern portion of the state is prairieland that is home to numerous lakes that support panfish populations.

For more information, contact the Division of Wildlife, 6060 Broadway, Denver, CO 80216.

Bluegills: Nee Noshe, Queens, Hasty, John Martin, Comanche, Horseshoe, Trinidad, Rio Blanco, Hollenbeck, Mack Mesa, Toften, McPhee, Navajo, Echo Canyon, Pastorius.

White Bass: Blue, La Junta, Boyd, Jackson, Prewitt, Sterling, Jumbo, Bonny, Nee Gronda, Horse Creek, Adobe, Nee Noshe, Queens, John Martin.

Yellow Perch: Boyd, Wellington, Boedecker, Lonetree, Carter, Lon Hagler, Barbour, Boulder, Jackson, Prewitt, Sterling, Jumbo.

Crappies: Northglen, CFI, Sterling, Julesberg, Pueblo, Wellington, Akron City, Lagerman, Boyd, Boedecker, Lonetree, Lon Hagler, Big Thompson, Barbour, Boulder, Seeley, Jackson, Prewitt.

Green Sunfish: Stalker.

CONNECTICUT

Connecticut is not the promised land for panfishermen. The state is small and its predominantly cold-water habitat favors trout. Nevethless, many panfish species grow large in Connecticut, especially chain pickerel and yellow perch.

For more information, contact the Department of Environmental Protection, Fisheries Division, 165 Capitol Ave., Hartford, CT 06106.

Yellow Perch: Black, Mashapaug, Waumgumbaug, East Twin, Candlewood, Beach, Moodus, Naubesatuck, Pataganset, Rogers, Saltonstall, Amos, Birge, Crystal, Gentiles, Hamilton, Tyler, Silvermine River.

Chain Pickerel: Wauregan, Mashapaug, Barkhamsted, East Twin, Naubesatuck, Pataganset, Rogers, Candlewood, Amos, Beaver Dam, Bog Meadow, Cedar, McDonough, Wononscoppomuc, Highland, Long, Moodus.

Bluegills: Mashapaug, Barkhamsted, East Twin, Saltonstall, Moodus, Naubesatuck, Waskewicz, Candlewood, Chaplin, Wheeler, Douning.

Rock Bass: Highland, Housatonic River.

Crappies: Barkhamsted, Saltonstall, Pataganset, Rogers, East Twin, Gardner.

Pumpkinseeds: Marie, Great, Housatonic River, Wononscoppomuc.

White Perch: Connecticut River, East Twin, Candlewood, Bantam, Lillionah, Saltonstall, Rogers, Squantz, Waramaug.

DELAWARE

Delaware is a bad news/good news state. The bad news is that, due to its small size, the state has very limited freshwater fishing opportunities. The good news is that what panfishing does indeed exist is of very high caliber. Most panfishing is done in state managed ponds ranging in size from 10 to 100 acres.

For more information, contact the Department of Natural Resources and Environmental

Delaware panfishing is of high caliber. But due to the small size of the state, most fishing is done in small, state-managed ponds up to 100 acres in size.

Control, Division of Fish & Wildlife, 89 Kings Highway, Dover, DE 19903.

White Perch: Red Mill, Augustine, Port Mahon, Bowers, Cedar, Little Assawoman, Nanticoke, St. Jones River, C & D Canal, Lewes, Phillips Landing.

Chain Pickerel: Horsey, Phillips Landing.

Yellow Perch: Milford, Red Clay, C & D Canal, Nanticoke River, Broad Creek, Phillips Landing.

Pumpkinseeds: Nanticoke River, Broad Creek, Milford.

Crappies: Milford, Noxntown, Nanticoke River, Broad Creek, Phillips Landing.

Bluegills: Milford, Red Mill, Nanticoke River, Broad Creek, Phillips Landing.

FLORIDA

The "Sunshine State" is especially favored by anglers seeking excellent winter fishing, but this shouldn't discourage a visit any time of year because outstanding panfishing is available during all 12 months.

For more information, contact the Game & Freshwater Fish Commission, 620 South Meridian St., Tallahassee, FL 32399.

Bluegills: Orange, Lochloosa, Panasoffkee, Rainbow River, Lake Blue Cypress, Tarpon, Istokpoga, Crystal, Crescent, Weir, Kissimmee, Tohopekaliga, George, Rodman, George, St.

John's River, Withlacoochee River, Chipola River, Alalachicola River, Talquin, Seminole.

Redear Sunfish: Orange, Panasoffkee, Lake Blue Cypress, Trafford, Tarpon, Istokpoga, Tsala Apopka, Crescent, Dora, Griffin, Harris, Yale, George, Rodman, Crystal River, St. John's River, Deer Point, Apalachicola River, Talquin, Wimico, Seminole, Jackson, Sopchoppy River, Choctawhatchee River, Lockloosa.

Crappies: South Lake, George, Okeechobee, Griffin, Kissimmee, Harris, Orange, Lochloosa, Lake Blue Cypress, Trafford, Tarpon, Tohopekaliga, St. John's River, Osborne.

Redbreast Sunfish: Panasoffkee, Rainbow River, Suwanee River, Chipola River, Blackwater River, Black Creek, Santa Fe River, Withlacoochee River, New River.

Warmouth: Orange, Guess, Lake Blue Cypress, Ocheesee, East River.

Chain Pickerel: Talquin, Iamonia.

White Bass: Apalachicola River.

GEORGIA

Georgia has 20 large, manmade reservoirs, 50,000 lakes and thousands of miles of streams and rivers. Nearly all of these waters are home to at least two or three different panfish species. Unfortunately, the state does not make available a list of which particular species are in each body of water. As with the few other states which likewise do not list such lakes, except for the purposes of indicating state record catches as indicated below, vacationing anglers should contact Chambers of Commerce offices in the specific areas they plan to visit.

For a pamphlet of fishing regulations and other information, contact the Department of Natural Resources, Game & Fish Division, 205 Butler St., SE, Atlanta, GA 30334.

White Bass: Lake Lanier

Bluegill: Shamrock Lake

Black Crappie: Lake Spivey

White Crappie: Brickyard Lake

Yellow Perch: Lake Burton

Redbreast Sunfish: Satilla River

Redear Sunfish: Ocmulgee River

IDAHO

Idaho is almost exclusively a cold-water trout and salmon state with very limited panfishing.

For more information, contact the Department of Fish & Game, 600 South Walnut St., Boise, ID 83707.

Yellow Perch: Wilson, Pend Oreille, Crothers.

Pumpkinseeds: Chase, Pend Oreille.

Bluegills: C.J. Strike

Crappies: Shepherd, Pend Oreille.

ILLINOIS

Illinois is primarily a very flat, agricultural state and as such has a minimum of rivers and streams. Most panfishing activities are conducted in lakes and reservoirs. Despite its land mass, panfishing opportunities in Illinois are well below the national average. Here are the best prospects.

Crappies: Chain of Lakes, Pierce, Shabbona, Lake of Egypt, Rend, Shelbyville, Crab Orchard, Mississippi River, Anderson, Clinton, Kinkaid, Decatur, Lou Yeager, Springfield, Vermillion, Mill Creek, Ohio River.

Bluegills: Chain of Lakes, Pierce, Shabbona, Lake of Egypt, Rend, Shelbyville, Crab Orchard, Mississippi River, Rock River, Baldwin, Devil's Kitchen, East Fork, Horseshoe, LaSalle, Mermet, Greenville/New City, Mill Creek.

White Bass: Baldwin, Chain of Lakes, Lake of Egypt, Rend, Shelbyville, Carlyle, Kaskaskia River, Mississippi River, Rock River, Heidecke, Illinois River, Decatur, La Salle, Powerton, Sangchris.

Yellow Perch: Arrowhead Club, Lake Michigan, Chain of Lakes, Horseshoe, Illinois River, Tampier, Wolf, Moses.

Rock Bass: Kankakee River, Auxsable Creek, Mississippi River.

Redear Sunfish: Dawson, Dutchman, Horseshoe, Mingo, Murphyboro, Mermet, Mill Creek, Sam Parr, Washington.

Yellow Bass: Carlyle, Charleston, Paradise, Maple, Wolf, Benton, Frankfort, Sesser, Gebhard.

INDIANA

The Hoosier State has abundant panfishing for numerous species. Local angling experts give the following lakes and rivers four-star ratings.

For more information, contact the Department of Natural Resources, Division of Fish & Wildlife, 402 W. Washington, Indianapolis, IN 46204.

Bluegills: Fox, James, Kickapoo, Minnehaha, Sullivan, Turtle Creek, Saddle, Grouse Ridge, Yellowwood, Freeman, Old, Indian, Koontz, Dogwood, Huntingburg, Patoka, Brookville, Celina, Manitou, South Mud, Morse.

Crappies: Grouse Ridge, Freeman, Dogwood, Huntingburg, Manitou, Brookville, South Mud, Gibson, Morse, Kokomo, Huntington, Salamonie, Brush Creek, Dewart.

Redear Sunfish: Grouse Ridge, Dogwood, Patoka, Manitou, Starve Hollow, Brush Creek, Big White Oak, Shock, Spear, Old, Pine, Stone, Griffy, Spring Valley.

Yellow Perch: Manitou, South Mud, Morse, Winona, Yellow Creek, Adams, Lake Michigan, Matinkuckee, Crooked, Loon, Sylvan, Glen Flint, Clear, James, Blue, Shriner.

White Bass: Freeman, Tippecanoe River, Brookville, South Mud, Kokomo, Huntington, Salmonie, Maxinkuckee, Mississinewa, Harden, Bass, Shafer, Ohio River.

Rock Bass: Tippecanoe River, Blue River, Maxinkuckee.

Longear Sunfish: Blue River.

IOWA

Iowa's landscape is mostly flat and agricultural. Yet annually it satisfies the appetites of 500,000 licensed anglers who visit the state's scores of natural lakes, manmade reservoirs, gravel pits, oxbow lakes, farm ponds, rivers and streams. Panfishing opportunities are both diverse and of high quality.

For more information, contact the Department of Natural Resources, Wallace State Office Bldg., Des Moines, IA 50319.

Crappies: Green Castle, Rathbun, Red Rock,

Storm, Clear, Coralville, Saylorville, Black Hawk, Five Island, North Twin, Badger, Big Creek, Carter.

Bluegills: Geode, Spirit, Okoboji, Clear, Browns, Cornelia, Little Spirit, Carter, Snyder, Badger, Big Creek, DeSoto Bend, Easter, Green Valley, Icaria.

White Bass: West Okoboji, Mississippi River, Spirit, Clear, Storm, Red Rock, Hartwick, Roberts Creek, Summit, Coralville, Rathbun.

Redear Sunfish: Meadow.

Yellow Perch: Spirit, West Okoboji, Ingham, Trumbull, West Swan, Anita.

Yellow Bass: Cedar River, Clear, North Twin, Arrowhead, Corning.

Rock Bass: Mississippi River

KANSAS

Panfishing in Kansas is rated excellent. Most of it is undertaken in large reservoirs, 21 of which dot the state, although many smaller lakes are also worth any angler's time.

For more information, contact the Department of Wildlife & Parks, Route 2, Pratt, KS 67124.

Crappies: Kirwin, Tuttle Creek, Wilson, Kanopolis, Pomona, John Redmond, Glen Elder, Keith Sebelius, Clinton, Milford, Council Grove, Hillsdale.

Bluegills, Redear Sunfish, Green Sunfish: Kanopolis, Milford, John Redmond, Keith Sebelius, Wilson, Webster Stilling, Antelope, Plainville, Hillsdale, Douglas, Geary, Miami, Osage, Ottawa, Shawnee, Olathe.

White Bass: Neosho River, Verdigris River, Ninnescah River, Spring River, Toronto, Fall River, Kanopolis, Milford, Pomona, Council Grove, Cheny, Cedar Bluff, Arkansas River.

Yellow Perch: Elbow.

KENTUCKY

In this angler's opinion, Kentucky represents the cradle of American panfishing. All but a few of the species described in this book can be caught in the Bluegrass State and quite often in very large numbers; the only exceptions are the white perch and yellow bass.

For more information, contact the Department of Fish & Wildlife Resources, Frankfort, KY 40601.

Crappies: Kentucky Lake, Barkley, Dale Hollow, Cumberland, Cave Run, Mill Creek, Grayson, Paintsville, Dewey, Fishtrap, Carr Fork, Ohio River, Herrington, Greenbo.

Bluegills, Redbreast Sunfish, Redear Sunfish, Longear Sunfish, Green Sunfish: Kentucky Lake, Barkley, Cumberland, Dale Hollow, Ohio River, Beaulah, Wood Creek, Paintsville, Laurel River, Dewey, Fishtrap, Buckhorn, Cave Run, Mill Creek, Herrington, Grayson, Taylorsville, Greenbo, Carter Caves.

White Bass: Kentucky Lake, Herrington, Fishtrap, Barren River, Barkley, Rough River, Nolin River, Green River, Dale Hollow, Cumberland, Buckhorn, Dewey.

Rock Bass: Casey Creek, Carter Caves, Mill Creek, Wood Creek.

Yellow Bass: Kentucky Lake.

Chain Pickerel: Clear, Beshear, Mauzy.

In Kentucky, the crappie is king, as this rather common stringer attests.

Warmouth: Dix River, Cannon Creek, Carpenter, Elmer Davis, Beshear, Malone, Mauzy, Shanty Hollow.

LOUISIANA

Not only does Louisiana offer year-around, open-water fishing, the bayou personality of the state yields what is best described as a nearly inexhaustible, untapped, fishing bonanza. Many of the sloughs and backwater swamps are unnamed and so vast that visiting anglers are well advised to hire local guides.

For more information, contact the Department of Wildlife & Fisheries, I & E Division, P.O. Box 98000, Baton Rouge, LA 70898.

Bluegills: Toledo Bend, Caddo, Mississippi River, False River, Atchafalaya.

Crappies: Toledo Bend, Caddo, Mississippi River, False River, Atchafalaya.

Redear Sunfish: Creston, Toledo Bend, Black, Bussey, D'Arbonne, Vernon, Mississippi River, Concordia, Saline-Larto, Spring Bayou, Atchafalaya.

White Bass: Toledo Bend, Mississippi River, Atchafalaya.

Warmouth: Florida Parishes.

Rock Bass: Florida Parishes.

Louisiana's panfishing is virtually untapped. The state has so much fishable water that most backwater sloughs and swamps are not even named.

MAINE

Maine is one of our finest fishing states, but not for panfish. Its latitude is more conducive to trout, salmon and northern pike. In small ponds and river drainages there is a marginal presence of white perch and chain pickerel, plus the two species are to be found in the following lakes.

For more information, contact the Department of Inland Fisheries & Wildlife, 284 State St., State House Station 41, Augusta, ME 04333.

White Perch: Messalonskee.

Chain Pickerel: Androscoggin.

MARYLAND

Considering its small size, Maryland is worth a second look when it comes to panfishing. Crappies, yellow perch and white perch are the main attractions, with the best catches usually coming from the state's various rivers.

For more information, contact the Forest, Park & Wildlife Service, Tawes State Office Bldg., Annapolis, MD 21401.

Crappies: Indian Acres, Higgins, Liberty, Pretty Boy, Loch Raven, Susquehanna River, Potomac River, Choptank River, Big Blackwater River, Wicomico Creek, Pocomoke, Depot Pond.

Yellow Perch: Deep Creek, Chesapeake Bay, Loch Raven, St. Mary's, Corsica River, Choptank River, Pocomoke.

White Perch: Dundee Creek, Garrison, Pretty Boy, Chester River, Wye River, Miles River, Choptank River, Big Blackwater River.

Bluegills: Jamieson, Stemmers, Higgins, Wicomico Creek.

Chain Pickerel: Johnson Pond, Cabin Creek, Warwick River, Hunting Creek, Broad Creek, Marshyhope.

MASSACHUSETTS

One of our smallest states, Massachusetts has limited panfish opportunities. The exception is the chain pickerel, which is found in virtually every lake, river and pond.

For more information, contact the Division of Fisheries and Wildlife, 100 Cambridge St., Boston, MA 02202.

Chain Pickerel: Pontoosuc, Benedict Pond, George, Pearl, Cheshire, Laurel, Onota, Plainfield, Forest, Boone, Congamond, Connecticut River, Quabbin, Massapoag.

Bluegills: Sportsmen's Ponds.

Yellow Perch: South Watuppa, Cape Cod Ponds, Quabbin.

White Perch: Quabbin.

Crappies: Jake's Pond.

MICHIGAN

With nearly 10,000 lakes within its borders, Michigan is a popular panfishing state. Add to this 12,500 miles of rivers and 1,700 miles of shoreline on the Great Lakes and it's clear that few other states offer the angler such a diversity of fishing opportunities.

For more information, contact the Fisheries Division, Michigan Department of Natural Resources, Box 30028, Lansing, MI 48909.

Bluegills, Crappies, Rock Bass, Longear Sunfish, Green Sunfish: Grand River, Lincoln, Kent, Houghton, Silver, Crooked, Autrian,

Michigan is one of our most popular panfishing states, during every month of the year!

Baldy, Fish, Miner, King, Vermilac, Deep, Middle, Marble, South Craig, Graham, Baldwin, Big Fish, LaGrange, Long, Paradise.

Yellow Perch: Lake St. Clair, Lake Michigan, Houghton, Eagle, Independence, Green, Fletcher, Long, Thunder Bay, Pine River, Whitney, Gun, Betsie, Big Paw Paw, Diamond, Burt, Emerson, Cisco.

White Bass: Thunder Bay, Van Etten, Sanford, Tittabawassee River, Saginaw Bay, Lake Erie, St. Clair, Detroit River.

MINNESOTA

Whoever first described Minnesota as the "Land of 10,000 Lakes" was dead wrong and the error has never been corrected. Actually, there are far more lakes and nearly all of them contain at least several panfish species. Yet in Minnesota the walleye is king and in his court are the northern pike, musky, smallmouth bass, largemouth bass and chinook salmon. Scant information is available from the state's fishery division regarding which specific panfish species are to be found in various waters.

For fishing regulations and other information, contact the Department of Natural Resources, Division of Fish & Wildlife, 500 Lafayette, St. Paul, MN 55155.

Crappies: Vermillion River, Minnetonka, Rainy, Lake of the Woods.

Bluegills: Alice, Mississippi River.

Yellow Perch: Plantaganette.

White Bass: St. Croix River, Minnesota River, Mississippi River, Cannon River, Zumbro River.

Yellow Bass: Mississippi River.

Green Sunfish: Charlotte.

Rock Bass: Lake Le Homme Dieu.

MISSISSIPPI

Being only 800 feet above sea level, there is little river or stream fishing in Mississippi, except in the river by that name and its many related oxbows and tributaries. Most panfishing opportunities are in lakes or Army Corps of Engineers reservoirs designed as flood-control impoundments.

For more information, contact the Department of Wildlife Conservation, Southport Mall, P.O. Box 451, Jackson, MS 39205.

Crappies: Ross Barnett, Enid, Grenada, Sardis, Pickwick, Tunica Cut-Off, Aliceville, Bay Springs, Columbus, Chotard, Whittington, Mississippi River.

Bluegills and Longear Sunfish: Grenada, Ross Barnett, Enid, Sardis, Pickwick, Tunica Cut-Off, Archusa.

Redear Sunfish: Horn, Legion, Tippah, Bay Springs, Pickwick, Divide Cut, Lamar Bruce, Old Natchez Trace, Jackson.

White Bass: Grenada, Yocona River, Enid, Yalobusha River, Bay Springs, Pickwick, Mississippi River, Big Black River, Okatibbee.

Warmouth: Black Creek, Big Black River, Bayou Pierre, Gin, Hamilton, Mike, Pearl River, Silver Creek, White Sand Creek, Bahala Creek, Tangipahoa River, Leaf River, Cammack Young, Bogue-Homa River, Okatoma River.

Yellow Bass: Horn, Mississippi River, Pearl River, Bayou Pierre, Rodney.

Chain Pickerel: Pickwick.

MISSOURI

The "Show-Me" state is a panfishing stronghold, which isn't difficult to understand when considering the abundance of fine waters—impounded and flowing—throughout the state but especially in the Ozark region.

For more information, contact the Department of Conservation, P.O. Box 180, Jefferson City, MO 65102.

Crappies: Table Rock, Stockton, Lake of the Ozarks, Wappapello, Taneycomo, Blue Springs, Bull Shoals, Truman.

Bluegills, Redear Sunfish, Longear Sunfish, Green Sunfish: Stockton, Lake St. Louis, Table Rock, Taneycomo, Lake of the Ozarks, Norfork.

White Bass: Bull Shoals, Lake of the Ozarks, Taneycomo, Thomas Hill, Jacomo, Long View, Norfork, Stockton, Table Rock, Truman, Lamine River, Pom de Terre River, Sac River.

Rock Bass: Big Piney River, Big River, Gasconade River, Meramec River, James River, Eleven Point River, North Fork White River, Castor River.

Yellow Perch: Butler City.

Chain Pickerel: Duck Creek.

MONTANA

Montana is almost exclusively a cold-water fishery with trout, grayling, northern pike and walleyes being the predominant species. Panfishing opportunities are very limited and restricted to small, shallow, privately owned ponds. The only two exceptions worth investigating, to which public access can be gained, are Dengel Reservoir and the Tongue River.

For more information, contact the Department of Fish, Wildlife & Parks, 1420 East Sixth Ave., Helena, MT 59620.

Bluegills: Dengel.

Crappies: Tongue River.

NEBRASKA

Sparsely populated Nebraska likes to claim that "it has more fish than fishermen" and with over

3,500 lakes and 11,000 miles of streams and rivers that may be very close to the truth. In any event, it is a very popular panfishing state.

For more information, contact the Game & Parks Commission, P.O. Box 30370, Lincoln, NE 68503.

Bluegills: Hackberry, Merritt, Grove, Swanson, Rock Creek, Wellfleet, Ft. Kearny, Elwood, Arnold, Sandy Channel, Ansley, Iron Horse Trail, Rockford, Bluestem, Branched Oak, Zorinzky, Wehrspann, Box Butte, Island, Oliver, Calamus, Clear, Dewey, Pelican, Big Alkali.

White Bass: Gavins Point, Harlan, Merritt, Maloney, Sherman, McConaughy, Swanson, Red Willow, Jeffrey, Medicine Creek, Johnson, Gallagher, Canyon, Midway Canyon, Sutherland, Republican River, North River, Glen Cunningham, Minatare, Lewis & Clark, Missouri River.

Crappies: Red Willow, Shoup, Harlan, Johnson, Sherman, Swanson, Lewis & Clark, Whitney, Enders, Rock Creek, Hayes Center, Wellfleet, Ansley, Medicine Creek, Elwood, Gallagher Canyon, Midway Canyon, Bluestem, Wehrspann, Box Butte, Minatare, Island, Oliver, Calamus, Willow, Goose, Missouri River.

Yellow Perch: Hackberry, Cody, Merritt, Enders, McConaughy, Ogallala, Elwood, Sutherland, Branched Oak, Box Butte, Minatare, Winters, Island, Oliver, Calamus, Clear, Dewey, Pelican, Big Alkali, Willow, Swan, Fremont.

Redear Sunfish: Rock Creek, Iron Horse Trail.

Rock Bass: Sandy Channel, Pawnee Slough, Iron Horse Trail.

Pumpkinseeds: Box Butte.

White Perch: Wagon Train.

NEVADA

Most panfishing opportunities in Nevada are restricted to Lake Mead and other large impoundments.

For more information, contact the Department of Wildlife, P.O. Box 10678, Reno, NV 89520.

White Bass: Lahontan, Harmon, Rye Patch, Sheckler, Stillwater, Wall Canyon, Mohave.

Bluegills: Hunewill, Humboldt River, Airport, Wildhorse, Mead, East Drain, Walker River, Warm Springs, Harmon, Lahontan, Pyramid, Rye Patch, Sheckler, Truckee River, Virginia, Mohave.

Crappies: Mead, Lahontan, Harmon, Rye Patch, Sheckler, Walker River, Weber, Humboldt River, Mohave.

NEW HAMPSHIRE

New Hampshire's mountainous landform sees the presence of mostly cold-water lakes and streams more conducive to salmonids than warmwater panfish species. The two primary panfishes in the state are the chain pickerel and white perch.

For more information, contact the Fish & Game Department, 2 Hazen Dr., Concord, NH 03301.

Chain Pickerel: Plummer, Akers, Airport, Beaver, Bow, Cedar, Copps, Crystal, Dan Hole, Granite, Winnepesaukee, Winnisquam.

White Perch: Goose, Squam, Mascoma, Massebesic, Ayers, Baboosic, Baker, Bow, Chocorua, Connecticut River, Eel Pond, Gorham, Great East, Halfmoon, Harvey, Highland, Kanasatka, Lovell, Merrimack River, Winnipesaukee, Willard, Winnisquam.

Yellow Perch: Head's Pond, Winnipesaukee, Winnisquam.

Crappies: Arlington Mill, Balch, Canobie, Clement, Crystal, Horseshoe, Lovewell, Scobie, Merrimack River, Otternick, Robinson.

Bluegills and Rock Bass: Connecticut River.

NEW JERSEY

One of our most populous states, New Jersey continues to offer excellent panfishing in selected waters.

For more information, contact the Department of Environmental Protection, Division of Fish, Game & Wildlife, CN-400, Trenton, NJ 08625.

Yellow Perch: Crosswicks Creek, Weequahic, Corbin City, Union, Round Valley, Carnegie, Farrington, Budd, Hopatcong, Musconetcong, Clinton, Greenwood, Monksville, Oak Ridge, Wanaque, Canistear, Swartswood.

Bluegills, Longear Sunfish, Pumpkinseeds, Green Sunfish, Redbreast Sunfish: Oradell, Laurel, Union, Weequahic, Round Valley, Spruce Run, Corbin City, Mercer, Farrington, Assunpink, Deal, Budd, Hopatcong, Musconetcong, Clinton, Greenwood, Echo.

Chain Pickerel: Aetna, Corbin City, Oradell, Mirrow, Tuckahoe, Union, Mercer, Assunpink, Clinton, Greenwood, Monksville, Wanaque, Canistear, Hopatcong.

White Perch: Hopatcong, Carnegie, Swartswood, Wanaque.

Rock Bass: Hopatcong.

Crappies: Forans, Bass, Mirrow, Union, Carnegie, Farrington, Mercer, Assunpink, Deal.

NEW MEXICO

Despite its spartan, desert appearance, New Mexico has a surprising number of panfishing opportunities, with 40,000 acre Elephant Butte Reservoir heading the list.

For more information, contact the Department of Game & Fish, State Capitol, Villagra Bldg., Santa Fe, NM 87503.

White Bass: Elephant Butte, Caballo, Avalon, Brantley, Sumner, Maxwell, Pecos River, Red Bluff, Rio Grande, Ute.

Bluegills: Elephant Butte, Lovington, Cochiti, Conchas, Harroun, Sumner, Navajo.

Crappies: Elephant Butte, Ute, Conchas, Abiquiu, Brantley, Caballo, Cochiti, Navajo, Santa Rosa, Storrie.

Longear Sunfish: Elephant Butte.

Yellow Perch: Elephant Butte, Miami, Charette.

NEW YORK

New York boasts 4,000 lakes and more than 70,000 miles of rivers and streams. Add to this the fact that the state borders on two of the Great Lakes (Ontario and Erie) and it's easy to understand why New York's panfishing is exceptional.

For more information, contact the Department of Environmental Conservation, Fish & Wildlife Division, 50 Wolf Rd., Albany, NY 12233.

Yellow Perch: Cayuga, Ontario, Erie, Oneida, Sececa, St Lawrence River, Delaware River, Hudson River, Mohawk River, Susquehanna River, Cassadaga, Chautauqua, Canandaigua, Champlain, East Branch, Pepacton, Schoharie, Sacandaga, Indian River, George, Long,

Although New York's lake fishing is excellent, many overlook its 70,000 miles of streams and rivers where panfishing action is equally superb.

Saranac, Meacham, Piseco, Raquette, Schroon, Tupper.

Bluegills, Redbreast Sunfish, Longear Sunfish, Pumpkinseeds: Wilds Pond, Delaware River, Hoosic River, Hudson River, Mohawk River, Peconic River, Schoharie Creek, Susquehanna River, Wall Kill, Amawalk, Ashokan, Cross River, Croton Falls, East Branch, Chautauqua, Cross, Erie, Ontario, Oneida, Cayuga, Tupper, Conesus, Seneca, Champlain, Placid, Pleasant, Long, Lincoln, Saranac, Loon, Paradox, Peck, Piseco, Raquette, Schroon.

Crappies: Chautauqua, St. Lawrence River, Indian, Black, Cross, Honeoye, Champlain, Otisco, Saratoga, Hoosic River, Hudson River, Susquehanna River, Bear, Findley, Ontario, Lamoka, Oneida, Cayuga, Keuka, Sacandaga, Paradox.

Chain Pickerel: Waneta, Lamoka, Tully, Greenwood, DeRuyter, Cauga, Toronto, Champlain, Delaware River, Hudson River, Peconic River, Susquehanna River, Oneida, Canandaigua, Pepacton, Titicus, West Branch, Canadarago, Greenwood, Otsego, Swinging Bridge.

Rock Bass: Catskill Creek, Delaware River, Hoosic River, Hudson River, Mohawk River, Schoharie Creek, Susquehanna River, Chautaqua, Cross, Erie, Ontario, Lamoka, Waneta, Oneida, Redfield, Cayuga, Hemlock, Honoeye, Keuka, Otisco, Owasco.

White Perch: Catskill Creek, Hudson River, Mohawk River, Peconic River, Cross, Erie, Ontario, Oneida, Otisco, Amawalk, Cross River, Croton Falls, East Branch, Kensico, Muscoot, New Croton, Titicus, West Branch, Placid.

White Bass: Oneida, Erie, Chautauqua, Ontario.

NORTH CAROLINA

North Carolina has the distinction of being mountainous in the west, gently rolling in the central part of the state, flat in the east, and offering a myriad of panfishing opportunities in all three regions.

For more information, contact the Wildlife Resources Commission, 512 N. Salisbury St., Raleigh, NC 27611.

Bluegills: Edneyville, Albemarle Sound, Waccamaw, Pamlico Sound, Tillery, W.K. Scott, Sutton, Rhodhiss, Roanoke River, New River, Lower Neuse River, South River, Black River, Cape Fear River, Brandt, Farmer, High Point, Holt, Hunt, Lucas, Michael, Oak Hollow, Reese.

Crappies: Asheboro City, Hickory, Tillery, Waccamaw, W. Kerr Scott, Sutton, Rhodhiss, Norman, New River, Merchants Millpond, B. Everett Jordan, Fontana, Chowan River, Blewett Falls, Hamlet City.

Redear Sunfish: Lee, Tillery, Waccamaw, Sutton, Roanoke River, Lower Neuse River, Merchants Millpond, Hickory, Contentnea, Cammack, Farmer, Hunt, Michael, Oak Hollow, Quaker Creek, Ramseur, Reese, Old Roxboro, Siler City.

Redbreast Sunfish: Tillery, Sutton, Rhodhiss, Roanoke River, New River, Lower Neuse River, James, Hickory, Contentnea, Lucas, Waccamaw River.

Pumpkinseeds: Waccamaw, Sutton, Rhodhiss, South River, Lower Neuse River, Hickory, Black River, Highpoint, Holt, Lucas, Oak Hollow.

Chain Pickerel: Merchants Millpond, Contentnea, Gum Swamp, Hamlet City, Ledbetter, Lumber River, South River, Black River, Cammack, Gaston.

White Bass: Fontana, Lookout Shoals, James, Tillery, Hickory, W. Kerr Scott, Blewett Falls, Badin.

Yellow Perch: Jones, Albemarle Sound, Pamlico Sound, Phelps, Waccamaw, Holt.

White Perch: Albemarle Sound, Tillery, Waccamaw, Roanoke River, Phelps, Chowan River, Badin, Gaston, Holt.

Rock Bass: New River.

Warmouth: Richmond, Sutton, Rhodhiss, Roanoke River, Hickory, South River, Black River.

NORTH DAKOTA

North Dakota is not home to a wide variety of panfish species. But the perch, crappie, and bluegill fishing is rated excellent.

For more information, contact the Game & Fish Department, 100 N. Bismarck Expressway, Bismarck, ND 58501.

Yellow Perch: Devils, Darling, Ashtabula, Wood, Metigoshe, Long, Pelican, Bowman, Gascoyne, Spring, Powers, Shimshek, Mitchell, New Johns, Tschida, Red Willow, Larson, Silver, Crystal Springs, Isabel, Williams, Kalmbach, LaMoure, George, Coldwater, Crooked, Audubon, Clearwater, White Earth, Nelson, Sand, Else.

Crappies: James River, Ashtabula, Tschida, Bowman, Metigoshe, Brekken, Audubon, Else, Silver, Cedar, Golden, Pipestem, Hiddenwood, Heart River, Cannonball River, Knife River,

Cedar River, Sheyenne River.

Bluegills: Strawberry, Jamestown, Mirror, Long, Clausen Springs, Ashtabula, Moon, Wood, Bowman, Spring, Mitchell, Tschida, Red Willow, Williams, Coldwater, Brekken, Crooked, Else, White Earth, Clearwater, Nelson, Cedar, Silver, Patterson, Golden, Jamestown, Pipestem, Armourdale, Hiddenwood, Rice, Tioga.

White Bass: Sakakawea, Ashtabula, Tschida, Metigoshe.

OHIO

Ohio is blessed with two top-notch fisheries, Lake Erie to the north and the Ohio River to the south. In between, the Buckeye State boasts hundreds of superb waters, each of which contains at least several panfish species.

For more information, contact the Department of Natural Resources, Division of Wildlife, 1840 Belcher Dr., Columbus, OH 43224.

Bluegills, Redear Sunfish, Pumpkinseeds: Lake Erie, Buckeye, Acton, Bressler, Ferguson, Findlay, Killdeer, LaSuAn, Nettle, Mogadore, Portage Lakes, Punderson, Tappan, Burr Oak, Dillon, Jackson, Alma, Logan, Salt Fork, Tycoon, Wellston, Rocky Fork, Rush Run, Stonelick, Muskingum Lakes.

Crappies: Buckeye, Ohio River, Delaware, Lake Erie, Auglaize River, Beaver Creek, Deer Creek, Charles Mill, Clear Fork, Delta, Harrison, Griggs, Lost Creek, Maumee River, Metzger Marsh, Nettle, Indian, New London, Pleasant Hill, Portage River, Muskingum Lakes, Sandusky River, Mogadore, Portage Lakes, Pymatuning, Action, Highlandtown, Mosquito, Kiser, Salt Fork, Seneca, Wellston, Rush Creek, Rocky Fork, Grand Lake.

Yellow Perch: Erie, Pymatuning, Bressler, Ferguson, Findlay, Killdeer, Lima, Lost Creek, Metzger Marsh, New London, Wauseon, Beaver Creek, LaComte, Paulding, Powers, Van Wert, Willard, Oberlin, Mosquito, Tappan, Barnesville, Dillon.

White Bass: Erie, Sandusky River, Maumee River, Ohio River, Bressler, Clear Fork, Ferguson, Huron River, Pleasant Hill, Portage River, Van Wert, Wauseon, Berlin, Milton, Mosquito, Pymatuning, Tappan, Dillon, Seneca, Buckeye, Delaware, Hoover, Indian.

Chain Pickerel: Long, Grand River, North, Zepernick, Zoar.

OKLAHOMA

Despite its dry, prairie terrain, panfishing action abounds in Oklahoma, which has close to 900,000 surface acres of water in the form of lakes and reservoirs. In fact, the state fish is the white bass.

For more information, contact the Department of Wildlife Conservation, 1801 N. Lincoln, Oklahoma City, OK 73105.

White Bass: Canton, Ft. Supply, Hudson, Sooner, Oologah, Tenkiller, Grand, Kaw, Ft. Gibson, Eufaula, Robert Kerr, Hugo, Broken Bow, Arbuckle, Murray, Texoma, Foss, Tom Steed, Lawtonka, Waurika, Clear Creek, Verdigris River.

Crappies: Canton, Ft. Supply, Hulah, Copan, Ft. Gibson, Oologah, Webbers Falls, Grand, Keystone, Hugo, Wister, Eufaula, Arbuckle, McGee Creek, Waurika, Chickasha, Tom Steed, Lawtonka, Ellsworth, Tenkiller, Lake O' the Cherokees.

Bluegills, Longear Sunfish, Green Sunfish, Redear Sunfish: American Horse, Elmer, Pretty

Walker, Claremore, Stilwell, Sallisaw, Spavinaw, Raymond Gary, Wayne Wallace, Murray, Wintersmith Park, Hall, Purcell, Burtschi, Tenkiller, Eufaula, Lake O' the Cherokees, Ft. Gibson.

Chain Pickerel: Logan Pond.

OREGON

Oregon has over 1,000 lakes and its temperate climate allows one kind of open-water fishing or another on a year-around basis. Although this is primarily a trout fishing state, panfishing opportunities are plentiful.

For more information, contact the Department of Fish & Wildlife, P.O. Box 59, Portland, OR 97207.

Crappies: Lost River, Gerber, Owyhee, Phillips, Hart, Thief Valley, Unity, Willamette Slough, Blind Slough, Drews, Cullaby, Westport Slough, Beaver Slough, Agate, Siltcoos, Clatskanie Slough.

Yellow Perch: Brownsmead, Brownlee, Blind Slough, Sunset, Cullaby, Grizzly Slough, Rilea Slough, Santosh Slough, Sauvie Island, Horsfall, Fords Mill, Tahkenitch, Gerber, Klamath.

Bluegills and Pumpkinseeds: Brownlee, Willamette Slough, Grizzly Slough, Sauvie Island, Tenmile, Fords Mill, Galesville, Tahkenitch, Warm Springs, Button Pond, Emigrant, Haystack, Selmac, Gerber, Round Valley, Drews, Siltcoos, Delta, Triangle, Rufus Slough.

Warmouth: Willamette River.

PENNSYLVANIA

The Keystone State is vastly different from one region to the next. Mountain ranges, riverbottoms, plateaus, and flatlands punctuate the landscape, providing a rich tapestry of fishing opportunities. It's a huge state, known mainly for its trout and salmon fishing, but the panfisherman can find a wealth of action as well. Unfortunately, since a majority of the thousands of lakes are relatively small, the state does not make available a listing of each specific species inhabiting each body of water; the chain pickerel is the only exception. Therefore, it is necessary for a visiting angler to ferret out panfishing prospects on his own by contacting Chamber of Commerce and tourism agencies in the particular locale he desires to fish.

For more information, contact the Fish Commission, P.O. Box 1673, Harrisburg, PA 17105.

Chain Pickerel: Shohola, Beechwood, Briar Creek, Carey, Fords, Cowanesque, Francis Slocum, Hammond, Heart, Hills Creek, Lackawanna, Montrose, Mountain, Quaker, Stump, Tingley, Tioga.

Yellow Perch: Wineola, Erie, Pymatuning.

Crappies: Pinchot, Erie, Pymatuning.

Bluegills: Trout, Erie, Pymatuning.

Rock Bass: Elk Creek, Erie.

RHODE ISLAND

Despite the fact that Rhode Island is both our smallest and most densely populated state, panfishing is not as limited as one may think.

For more information, contact the Department of Environmental Management, Division of Fish & Wildlife, 4808 Tower Hill Rd., Wakefield, RI 02879.

Bluegills: St. Mary's Pond, Bowdish, Johnson, Pascoag, Quidnick, Slack, Smith & Sayles, Stafford, Tiogue, Wallum, Waterman, Worden.

Chain Pickerel: Stafford, Worden, Beach, Johnson, Indian, Oak Swamp, Pascoag, Ponagansett, Quidnick, Slack, Smith & Sayles, Tiogue, Wallum, Watchaug, Waterman, Woonsocket, Yawgoog.

Yellow Perch: Bowdish, Johnson, Indian, Oak Swamp, Pascoag, Ponagansett, Quidnick, Slack, Smith & Sayles, Stafford, Tiogue, Wallum, Watchaug, Waterman, Woonasquatucket, Woonsocket, Worden, Yawgoog.

White Perch: Tucker, Indian, Oak Swamp, Quidnick, Waterman, Worden.

Pumpkinseeds: Beach, Bowdish, Johnson, Indian, Oak Swamp, Pascoag, Ponagansett, Quidnick, Stafford, Tiogue, Wallum, Watchaug, Waterman, Woonsocket.

Crappies: Watchaug, Beach.

SOUTH CAROLINA

The Palmetto State's most highly touted fish species are the largemouth bass and striped bass. Unfortunately, although panfishing opportunities are nothing short of excellent, the state does not make available a listing of which particular species inhabit various waters; the exception has to do with state records taken from the following waters. Visiting anglers should contact the state's many regional tourism agencies.

For more information, contact the Wildlife and Marine Resources Department, P.O. Box 167, Columbia, SC 29202.

White Bass: Lake Wylie.

Black Crappie: Lipsey's Landing.

White Crappie: Lake Murray.

Yellow Perch: Lake Keowee.

White Perch: Lake Murray.

Chain Pickerel: Lake Marion.

Pumpkinseed: Lake Moultrie.

Redbreast Sunfish: Lumber River.

Warmouth: Douglas Swamp.

SOUTH DAKOTA

South Dakota's gem is the Missouri River, which encompasses 900 square miles of panfishing water. It is an extremely fertile fishery. In fact, 24 of the state's record fish were taken from the Missouri or one of the various reservoirs created along the river's length. Many other lakes and rivers provide still additional panfishing opportunities.

For more information, contact the Department of Game, Fish & Parks, Anderson Bldg., Pierre, SD 57501.

Crappies: Oahe, Ft. Randall, Lewis & Clark, Sheridan, Michell, Big Stone, Elm, Traverse, South Buffalo, Hendricks, Pelican, Byron, Richmond, Sand, Kampeska, Blue Dog, Enemy Swim, Pickerel, Alice, Bullhead, Clear, North Scatterwood, Thompson.

Yellow Perch: Mitchell, Sand, Big Stone, Henry, Traverse, Dam, Byron, Campbell, Hendricks, Thompson, Oakwood, Elm, Richmond, Andes, Willow, Brandt, Kampeska, Pelican, Punished Woman, Blue Dog, Herman, Enemy Swim, Pickerel, Minnewasta, Rush, Fish, Long, Waubay.

Bluegills: Mitchell, Big Stone, Richmond, Andes, Kampeska, Enemy Swim, Madison, Buffalo, Cochrane, Brandt, Herman, Yankton, Cottonwood.

Pumpkinseeds and Green Sunfish: Hayes, Carthage.

White Bass: Lewis & Clark, Enemy Swim, Mud, Kampeska, Orman, Pickerel.

Rock Bass: Enemy Swim, Kampeska, Blue Dog, Pickerel.

TENNESSEE

From the fertile delta plains where the western part of the state borders the Mississippi River to the rugged mountains of the east, Tennessee is a panfisherman's heaven. In fact, it is claimed that virtually every body of water within the state is home to at least three panfish species, and in some cases many more. Here are the best picks.

For more information, contact the Wildlife Resources Agency, P.O. Box 40747, Nashville, TN 37204.

Crappies: Reelfoot, Pickwick, Center Hill, Watts Bar, Norris, Old Hickory, Cherokee, Nick-a-Jack, Kentucky Lake, Percy Priest, Tim's Ford, Normandy, Dale Hollow, Cordell Hull, Tellico, Fort Loudon, Boone.

Bluegills: Old Hickory, Cherokee, Falls Creek, Reelfoot, Cheatham, Percy Priest, Normandy, Cordell Hull, Watts Bar, Norris, Nick-a-Jack, Tellico, Fort Loudon, Melton Hill, Kentucky Lake, Mississippi River, Woods, Tim's Ford, Dale Hollow.

Redbreast Sunfish: Holston River, Herb Parson's, Hatchie River, Duck River, Buffalo River, Cumberland River, Obey River, Harpeth River, Stones River, Clinch River, Nolichucky River, Sequatchie River.

White Bass: Kentucky Lake, Pickwick, Center Hill, Watts Bar, Parksville, Barkley, Dale Hollow, Norris, Stones River, Percy Priest, Fort

Loudon, Melton Hill, Cherokee, Douglas, Old Hickory.

Longear Sunfish: Pigeon River, Hatchie River, Duck River, Buffalo River, Cumberland River, Obey River, Harpeth River, Stones River, Clinch River, Nolichucky River, Holston River, Sequatchie River.

Chain Pickerel: Kentucky Reservoir.

Rock Bass: Stones River, Duck River, Buffalo River, Cumberland River, Obey River, Harpeth River, Clinch River, Nolichucky River, Holston River, Sequatchie River.

Yellow Bass: Reelfoot, Watts Bar.

Yellow Perch: Hiwassee.

Redear Sunfish: Carroll, Humboldt, Graham, Laurel Hill, Maples Creek, Marrowbone.

Warmouth: Pipkins, Nolinchucky River.

TEXAS

Texas fishery officials do not provide to the general public data regarding which specific species inhabit the Lone Star State's 800 panfishing lakes. Rather, the state is divided into eight geographical regions and the species inhabiting those regions are listed. Compounding the problem, many panfish species are to be found in all eight regions. Consequently, it is nearly impossible for an angler to know which particular species inhabit a given lake without seeking local advice. Following are the panfish species known to exist in the major reservoirs.

For more information, contact the Parks & Wildlife Department, 4200 Smith School Rd., Austin, TX 78744.

Bluegills, Redear Sunfish, Green Sunfish,

Redbreast Sunfish, Longear Sunfish: Caddo, Toledo Bend, Sam Rayburn, Livingston, Meredith, Texarkana, Amistad, Guadalupe River.

Crappies: Navarro Mills, Texarkana, Caddo, Toledo Bend, Sam Rayburn, Livingston, Amistad, Meredith, Lake of the Pines.

White Bass: Longhorn Dam, Texoma, Texarkana, Meredith.

Chain Pickerel: Caddo.

UTAH

Utah is primarily a trout and salmon state with very limited panfishing. Consequently, the state maintains a listing only of record fish taken in the scant number of waters where various panfish species have been introduced.

For more information, contact the Division of Wildlife Resources, 1596 West North Temple, Salt Lake City, UT 84116.

White Bass: Utah Lake.

Bluegills: Pelican Lake.

Black Crappie: Lake Powell.

VERMONT

Despite its small size and proximity to large population centers, Vermont offers excellent panfishing, usually in the midst of stunning mountain countryside.

For more information, contact the Fish & Wildlife Department, Waterbury, VT 05676.

Yellow Perch: Champlain, Memphremagog, Bomoseen, Dunmore, Hortonia, St. Catherine, Otter Creek, Connecticut River, Echo, Fairlee,

Morey, Harriman, Somerset, Carmi, Joes, Marshfield.

Chain Pickerel: Champlain, Fairlee, Morey, Connecticut River, Harriman, Somerset.

Bluegills: Barber's Pond, Somerset.

Pumpkinseeds: Lamoille River, Groton Pond.

Crappies: Charcoal Creek.

Rock Bass: Champlain.

VIRGINIA

Virginia's panfishing can only be described as so vast that an entire book could be devoted to this state alone. Eleven major river systems and their tributaries, hundreds of manmade impoundments, and scores of smaller lakes, indeed make Virginia a panfisherman's delight. Here are the best prospects well worth any angler's time.

For more information, contact the Department of Game & Inland Fisheries, 4010 W. Broad St., Richmond, VA 23230.

Crappies: Conner, Kerr, Anna, Chickahominy, Lee Hall, Diascund, Prince, Cohoon, Meade, Burnt Mills, Drummond, Gaston, Nottoway River, Blackwater River, South Holston, Northwest River, Smith Mountain, Abel.

Bluegills: Kerr, Chickahominy, Waller Mill, Diascund, Western Branch, Prince, Meade, Burnt Mills, Blackwater River, Amelia, Northwest River, North Landing River, Connor, Meherrin River.

Redbreast Sunfish, Redear Sunfish: Chickahominy, Waller Mill, Amelia, Pamunkey River, Western Branch, Prince, Cohoon, Meade, Nottoway River, Briery Creek, Connor, Appomattox River, James River, Philpott, Rivanna, Maury River, Cowpasture River, Burke, Shenandoah River.

Yellow Perch: New River, Potomac River, Anna, Chickahominy, Waller Mill, Mattaponi River, Pamunkey River, Rappahannock River, Western Branch, Burnt Mills, Drummond, Brunswick, Nottoway River, North Landing River.

White Perch: Potomac River, Chickahominy, Lee Hall, James River, Pamunkey River, Rappahannock River, Western Branch, Northwest River, North Landing River, Gaston, Anna, Occoquan, Motts Run, Back Bay.

Chain Pickerel: Douthat, Chickahominy, Anna, Waller Mill, Lee Hall, Diascund, Burnt Mills, Prince, Cohoon, Drummond, Gaston, Nottoway River, Blackwater River, Appomattox River, Abel.

White Bass: Occoquan, Kerr, Dan River, Bannister River, Smith Mountain, Leesville, Claytor, New River, Orange.

Rock Bass: Gaston, Nottoway River, New River, James River, Jackson River, Cowpasture River, Shenandoah River, Laurel Bed.

WASHINGTON

Washington is foremost a trout state, yet the panfisherman can find ample sport with yellow perch, bluegills, and crappies.

For more information, contact the Department of Wildlife, 600 Capitol Way N., Olympia, WA 98501.

Yellow Perch: Steilacoom, Columbia River, Dry, Lacamas, Vancouver, Horseshoe, Silver, Banks, Potholes, Soda, Green, Meridan, Sammamish, Sawyer, Alder, American, Spanaway,

Tanwax, Big Lake, Perch, Clear, Ki, Shoecraft, Stevens, Downs, Long, Newman, Deer, Waitts, Black, Offut, Patterson, Whatcom, Terrell.

Bluegills: Potholes, Columbia River, Lacamas, Horseshoe, Horsethief, Rifle, Newman, Loon, Long.

Crappies: Columbia River, Vancouver, Silver, Scooteney, Banks, Potholes, Horsethief, Riffe, Palmer, Alder, Clear, Spanaway, Tanwax, Big Lake, Eloika, Long, Newman, Deer, Black, Patterson.

Pumpkinseeds: Hicks, Dry, Sawyer, Tanwax, Long.

Rock Bass: Long, American, Patterson.

WEST VIRGINIA

West Virginia is a mountain state with few lakes and a profusion of rivers suitable only for trout and smallmouth bass. Less than 100 square miles of surface water is inhabited by panfish. Following are the best bets.

For more information, contact the Wildlife Resources Division, State Capitol Complex, Bldg. 3, Charleston, WV 25305.

Crappies: Meathouse Fork, Bluestone, Big Ditch, Kee, Little Beaver, Miletree, O'Brien, Plum Orchard, Ridenour.

Bluegills: Bluestone, Bear-Rocks, Berwind, Big Ditch, Boley, Brushy Fork, Kee, Little Beaver, O'Brien, Pipestem, Plum Orchard, Sherwood, Silcott-Fork, Watoga.

White Bass: Kanawha River, Bluestone, New River, Hawks Nest.

Rock Bass: Greenbrier River, Big Sandy, Hawks Nest.

Chain Pickerel: Back Creek, Fort Ashby.

Green Sunfish: Brushy Fork.

WISCONSIN

Wisconsin is known primarily for its clear, cold, glacial lakes and its stellar musky and walleye fishing, which means its panfish populations go largely unheralded. And that's just fine with those who recognize the state's potential for excellent panfish catches. Of Wisconsin's 8,700 lakes and thousands of miles of river systems, these are the best bets.

For more information, contact the Bureau of Wildlife Management, Box 7921, Madison, WI 53707.

Bluegills, Pumpkinseeds, Crappies, Yellow Perch, Green Sunfish, Rock Bass: Mississippi River, Squash, Rush, Winnebago, Winneconne, Wind, Bishop, Lac La Belle, Pewaukee, Butte Des Morts, Poygan, Minong Flowage, Shell, Spooner, Trego, Big Cedar, White Sand, Como, Beulah, Delavan, Whitewater, Presque Isle, Rest, Smoky, Star, Lac Court Oreilles.

White Bass: Wolf River, Winnebago, Mendota, Mississippi River, Monona, Waubesa, Okauchee.

WYOMING

Wyoming primarily supports cold-water fisheries not conducive to the requirements of most panfish species. Therefore, opportunities to catch the various species are minimal. Bluegills, crappies, sunfish and yellow perch are found only in scant numbers, mostly in private ponds. The only public panfishing opportunities are as follows.

For more information, contact the Game & Fish Department, Cheyenne, WY 82002.

Crappies: Grayrocks, Hawk Springs, Boysen.

Yellow Perch: Boysen.

Canada

Canada is synonomous with exceptionally high-quality fishing in literally billions of acres of fishable water. But their fisheries management devotes most of its attention and related record keeping to gamefish, and information on panfishing is scant and sometimes even nonexistent.

ALBERTA

Alberta is one such province in which its grayling and seven species of trout stand in the limelight. Only the yellow perch is mentioned in available fishing guidebooks.

For more information, contact the Fish and Wildlife Division, Petroleum Plaza, 9945–108 St., Edmonton, Alberta T5K 2G6.

Yellow Perch: Forty Mile Coulee Reservoir, Swartz Lake, Little Ruby, Moose.

BRITISH COLUMBIA

British Columbia is another province that is mecca to trout and salmon anglers. The two predominating panfish species are black crappies and yellow perch.

For more information, write to the Fish and Wildlife Branch, Parliament Buildings, Victoria, British Columbia V8V 1X5.

Black Crappie: Plentiful in some sloughs and backwaters of the Lower Fraser River and Lower Okanagan River.

Yellow Perch: Osoyoos Lake, Duck Lake, Sloughs of the Kootenay River, Swan Lake, Charlie.

ONTARIO

Ontario is within an easy day's drive of millions of anglers and if one tires of the superb walleye, pike, musky and smallmouth angling, one can easily switch to panfish, often in the very same body of water.

For more information, write to the Ministry of Natural Resources, 900 Bay St., Toronto, Ontario M7A 2C1.

Yellow Perch: Nipissing, Nipigon, Lake of the Woods, Lac Seul, Lac des Mille Lacs, Little Vermilion, St. Joseph, Albany, Burrows, Chipman, Wilcox, Essnagami, Fernow, Gamsby, Klotz, Long, O'Sullivan, Turkey, Twin, Wildgoose, Wintering, Jackinnes, Cedar, Fields, Hayes, Kagiano, Poppy, Whitefish, Bayfield, Big Skunk, Cameron, Fushimi, Hanian, Wolverine, Pigeon, Agnew, Birch, Manitou, Wolsey, French River, Belwood, Simcoe, Wagner, Georgian Bay, Gould, Canyon, Rugby, Thunder, Thadeus.

Crappies: All river tributaries and sheltered bays of the lower Great Lakes, Lake of the Woods, Namakan, Rainy, Sandpoint, Lake St. Francis, Consecon, Dog, Syndeham, Trent River, Wolfe, Simcoe, Gould, Wilcox.

Pumpkinseeds: Most clear, shallow, weedy waters south of Temagami.

Bluegills: All warm, vegetated, still waters throughout southern Ontario.

White Perch: Lake Ontario, Lake Erie, Rondeau Bay, Lower Niagara River.

White Bass: Clear waters near rock reefs and sand bars in the Lower Great Lakes area.

Rock Bass: all shallow, slow waters south of Lake Atitibi, Grand River, Wildwood.

MANITOBA

The only way to describe Manitoba is "virtually unlimited fishing opportunities." When you've limited-out with pike and walleyes on any given day, don't head back to the dock. Now begin filling your stringer with panfish.

For more information, write to Travel Manitoba, 155 Carlton St., Winnipeg, Manitoba R3C 3H8.

Yellow Perch: Winnipeg River, East Angling, Singush, Dorothy, Wintering, Gem, Pinawa, Lake of the Prairies, Eleanor, Goose, East Blue, Snow, Foot Print, Buffalo Bay, Big Whiteshell, Lee River, Cross, Wrong, Margaret, White, Nutimik, William, Pelican, Island.

Black Crappie: Star Lake, Winnipeg River, Minnewasta, Red River, Lake Winnipeg, Manigotagan River.

Rock Bass: Winnipeg River, Lake of the Prairies, St. Malo, Assiniboine River, Lee River, Lac Du Bonnet, Rat River, Shell River, Eaglenest, Wahtopaneh, Falcon, Maskwa, Bird, Saddle, Nutimik, North Cross.

White Bass: Red River, Winnipeg River, Assiniboine River, Manigotagan River, Lake Winnipeg, Nutimik.

NEW BRUNSWICK

Mention New Brunswick and the province's world-wide reputation for salmon fishing comes to mind. Panfishing is largely overlooked, but that doesn't mean it is inconsequential. Actually, four different panfish species are quite plentiful and worth any angler's time.

For more information, write to the Fish and Wildlife Branch, P.O. Box 6000, Fredericton, New Brunswick E3B 5H1.

Yellow Perch: St. Croix River, Red Rock, Sparks, Utopia, Teaques, Belvedere, Cooks, Charlie, Dicks, Eagle, Alva, Baker, First Green River, Glazier, Quisbis, Second Green River, Third Green River, Crocker, Holmes, Knoll Spruce, Mitchell, Remous, Rock Pond, Second Fowler, Big Nictin, Hicks, French, Indian, Gulquac, Long, Trousers, Square, Amelie.

White Perch: St. John River, Wheaton, Hart, Grand, Maquapit, French, Indian, Square, Amelie, Bolton, First Eel, Kelly Creek, Longs Creek, Mactaquac, Modsley, McAdam, North, Skiff, Spednic, Tomlinson, Woolastock.

Pumpkinseeds: St. John River, St. Croix River, Coronary, McDougall, Belvedere, Brunswick, Cassidy, Deer, Eagle, Little John, Robin Hood, Grand, French, Sunpoke, Burntland, First Eel, Modsley.

Redbreast Sunfish: St. John River, St. Croix River, Coronary, McDougall, Belvedere, Brunswick, Cassidy, Deer, Eagle, Little John, Robin Hood, Grand, French, Sunpoke, Burntland, First Eel, Modsley.

QUEBEC

Quebec boasts one million lakes and an unknown number of river systems. Unfortunately, the province keeps records pertaining only to pike, walleye, musky, landlocked salmon, Atlantic salmon, and splake. All other fish are lumped into an "other species" category. Therefore, in studying the province's fishing guidebook and seeing "other species" listed as inhabiting a particular body of water, they may be largemouth bass, smallmouth bass, panfish, catfish, or any combination of these species.

For more information, write to Ministere du Loisir, de la Chasse et de la Peche, 150, boul. Saint-Cyrille est, Quebec City, Quebec G1R 4Y1.

SASKATCHEWAN

Saskatchewan is yet another premier fishing province, best known for its walleye, pike, and smallmouth bass fishing. Unfortunately, the province does not keep records pertaining to which panfish species inhabit specific lakes.

The province does, however, have available splendid guidebooks with listings for hundreds of fishing camp outfitters, all of which are well aware of the specific species in their particular lakes. To receive these guidebooks and other fishing information, write to Tourism Saskatchewan, 1919 Saskatchewan Dr., Regina, Saskatchewan S4P 3V7.